HOUSEHOLD
HINTS

HOUSEHOLD
HINTS

Random Little Library
an imprint of
Random House Australia Pty Ltd
20 Alfred Street, Milsons Point NSW 2061

Sydney New York Toronto
London Auckland
and agencies throughout the world

Series Co-ordination: Gordon Cheers
Design: Liz Nicholson, Design Bite
Typeset by Axiom, 139 Charles Street, Abbotsford Vic 3067
Production by Vantage Graphics, Sydney
Printed by Australian Print Group, Maryborough

ISBN 0 09 182807 4

CONTENTS

COMMON STAINS

Your household stain-tackling kit should include such basic items as clean white absorbent cloths, white vinegar, kitchen salt, mild dishwashing liquid (a neutral cleaner), bicarbonate of soda (baking soda), cloudy ammonia (be careful not to inhale the fumes), lemons, talcum powder, carpet shampoo, methylated spirit, dry cleaning fluid and eucalyptus oil (available from chemists and hardware stores).

In your laundry you will have an enzyme detergent and pre-wash treatment, and a laundry bleach (this contains chlorine — don't inhale the fumes). Buy other proprietary preparations only as you need them.

Read the directions carefully on the bottles of all chemicals before you use them. Always test first on a part of the fabric or carpet that doesn't show. Use minimal amounts of chemicals. Dab on stains, don't flood them and, where possible, have a pad underneath the stain when you are treating it.

If in doubt get professional advice, and remember that it is important to deal with most stains quickly.

Acid *(urine, vinegar or stronger acids such as bleach)*

Soak with water quickly, then neutralise acid spills immediately with a strong solution or paste of bicarbonate of soda and water, or cloudy ammonia and water (one part ammonia to two parts water).

Adhesives

As there are so many different adhesives, the best idea is to ask about removal methods when you buy. If in doubt, ring the manufacturer.

Beer

Rinse beer stains from washable articles in cold water with a tablespoon or two of white vinegar added, then wash in hot water as normal.

Beer stains on carpet and upholstery can be removed by sponging with a weak solution of a few drops of white vinegar and liquid dishwashing detergent in cold water.

Beetroot

Washable fabrics should be rinsed in cold water as soon as possible and then soaked in detergent. Sponge non-washable articles with cold water.

Blood

Soak fresh bloodstains on washable fabrics in cold salt water for as long as possible before washing.

A cold soak in an enzyme detergent or a tablespoon of cloudy ammonia added to the washing water will help to thoroughly cleanse the article. Do not use ammonia on synthetics or delicates.

Sponge bloodstains on carpets with soda water and blot up as much moisture as possible. Follow up with a carpet shampoo.

Sponge bloodstains on non-washable articles with a weak solution of cloudy ammonia in cold water. Blot well.

In all cases, dried blood-stains need professional help.

Candle wax

Make sure the wax is hard before you try to remove it from fabrics, carpets or upholstery. Use ice cubes in a pack to freeze it if necessary. Then chip the wax away. If there is a grease mark, cover it with talcum powder and leave for several hours. Repeat this several times. As a last resort, dab remaining grease spots with dry cleaning fluid or eucalyptus oil.

Chewing gum

To remove chewing gum from carpets, use a freeze preparation, available from hardware stores. Spray on the gum; it will harden and you can then break into small pieces and collect or vacuum it up. An alternative is to use ice cubes in a plastic bag to do the hardening. To finish the job, sponge with a mild neutral cleaner (such as dishwashing liquid) in warm water.

Eucalyptus oil will also remove chewing gum from carpets — and from children's hair!

Chocolate
Remove all solids. Sponge washable fabrics with soda water, or soak in an enzyme pre-wash treatment before warm washing. If stain persists try a tablespoon of cloudy ammonia in the wash water.

Try soda water on upholstery and carpets, then sponge with a solution of warm water and cloudy ammonia.

Coffee and tea
Fresh coffee and tea stains on washable fabric can usually be sponged out with tepid or cold water or weak bicarbonate of soda solution. (Hot water may set the stains.) Soak in pre-wash treatment if necessary and launder in an enzyme detergent.

Do not use ammonia on tea and coffee stains.

Old tea and coffee stains must be soaked in an enzyme detergent.

Black coffee stains on washable fabrics often respond to rinsing with soda water.

Tea and coffee stains on carpet and upholstery should be sponged with water then a weak solution of white vinegar and dish-washing liquid in water or bicarbonate of soda and water.

Correction fluid
Be careful not to tear fabrics when attempting to scrape off dried correction fluid. Allow the fluid to dry before attempting to remove it.

Nail polish remover (acetone, not oily) can be used on hardy fabrics to remove the stain. Dry clean synthetics or wool.

Egg
Never use hot water on egg stains. Get the stain out before washing.

Sponge with cold salt water. Washable fabrics can be soaked in an enzyme pre-wash treatment and then laundered in tepid water.

Use a solution of dishwashing liquid and a few drops of white vinegar to remove egg stains from carpets and upholstery. Blot dry.

Faeces
Remove solids, then sponge with solution of white

vinegar and dishwashing liquid in warm water. Washables may be laundered in an enzyme detergent, or a little cloudy ammonia may be added to the wash water for hardy fabrics and work clothes.

Fruit and fruit juice

Fruit stains on washable fabrics should be sponged immediately with soda water or a cold bicarbonate of soda and water solution. Heat will set the stains. Soak in cold pre-wash treatment before washing normally. An enzyme washing powder may help.

Lift fruit juice stains off non-washable fabrics by covering with salt or bicarbonate of soda. Allow the salt to absorb the liquid, brush off and repeat if necessary.

Sponge dry stains with cold water, or a solution of bicarbonate of soda and cold water. When dry, you may need to use dry cleaning fluid to spot.

Grass

Grass stains on washable fabrics should be dabbed with methylated spirit or soaked in an enzyme detergent and cold water or laundry bleach and cold water (follow manufacturer's instructions) before washing. If you are using bleach, test the fabric first. Dab non-washable fabrics with methylated spirit to remove grass stains — but test the fabric first.

Eucalyptus oil will lift grass stains from washable fabrics.

Grease and oil

Grease marks can be lifted from most fabrics using talcum powder.

Use plain white talc, cover the spot and leave for at least 30 minutes before dusting off. Repeat the process if necessary.

Tailors' chalk and cornmeal are alternative absorbent lifters for grease marks.

When treating grease stains have a pad of clean fabric underneath the stain. Change the pad when the stain moves on to it.

Another method of dealing with grease and oil is to place brown or blotting paper over the spot and rub the paper with a warm iron.

This will lift the grease on to the paper. Repeat this several times, moving the paper to absorb more grease. Washable fabrics can then be soaked in pre-wash treatment and laundered.

Dry cleaning fluid can be used to remove grease and oil marks from carpets and upholstery. Use small amounts to avoid making ring marks.

Use dry cleaning fluid to spot grease marks on non-washable fabrics, but don't use it on synthetics. Try the talcum method instead and get professional help if necessary.

Eucalyptus oil will remove grease from wool and leather. Dab gently on the spot.

Ink
(ballpoint)
Ink may be removed from washable fabrics by spotting with methylated spirit. Rinse then wash normally in hot water.

Another treatment is to sponge the stain with milk, then rinse in cool water before washing.

Dab ink spilled on carpet with methylated spirit or squirt with hair spray, then sponge with a solution of warm water and a few drops of dishwashing liquid and white vinegar.

Kitchenware care
A paste of bicarbonate of soda left on overnight will lift burned food from cookware.

Remove stains on aluminium and cast iron saucepans by boiling a solution of white vinegar and water in them.

Apple peelings or rhubarb leaves boiled in aluminium saucepans will also remove stains.

Boil a solution of bicarbonate of soda, a little household bleach and water in non-stick cookware to remove stains.

Wash thoroughly and smear with cooking oil after treatment.

Badly stained Pyrex dishes can be rejuvenated by soaking in household bleach. Wash thoroughly after treatment.

Bad tea stains can be removed from cups and china teapots by scrubbing with kitchen salt.

Remove fish and onion odours from cookware (and your hands) by rubbing with a cut lemon.

Leather treatments

Scuff marks on white shoes, belts and bags can be camouflaged with white correcting fluid.

Rub worn and dull leather shoes and surfaces with beaten egg white to rejuvenate shine.

Dab eucalyptus oil on grease spots on leather shoes before you clean them, or try talcum powder left on the spots for an hour or so.

For grease stains on leather furniture, try absorbing as much as possible with talcum powder.

Lipstick *(and shoe polish)*

Remove any solids.

Washable fabrics can be dabbed with methylated spirit — but use great care.

Use dry cleaning fluid on upholstery and non-washable fabrics.

Liquids

When any liquid is spilled, the most urgent job is to blot up as much as possible. Cover the fluid with a towel or soft cloth and press hard to absorb it.

Marble

Two or three tablespoons of cloudy ammonia in water is a good general cleaner for marble.

Try lemon juice to remove stains from marble surfaces, but rinse off quickly as the acid in the juice will bleach the stone.

Never put oily polish or wax on white marble — it may discolour it.

Marks on vinyl

White toothpaste on a cloth will take black scuff marks off vinyl floors. Rub lightly. As it is only a light abrasive, the toothpaste will not harm the finish.

Mildew

Rub washable fabrics with lemon juice and salt and bleach in the sun to remove mildew spots. Rinse and launder in an enzyme detergent.

Yellowed or mildewed white cotton or damask fabrics can be rejuvenated by soaking in a weak solution of laundry bleach (follow manufacturer's directions) for an hour or two. Rinse and wash as normal.

Milk

Milk stains on washable fabrics can be removed by a cold water soak with a few drops of ammonia added to the water. Or you could use

a pre-wash treatment. Rinse and then launder in an enzyme detergent in tepid water.

Milk on carpet and non-washables should be sponged with soda water immediately and then with dishwashing liquid in warm water. Rinse spots with cool water and blot all liquid carefully.

Keep water tepid or cool when dealing with milk stains. Hot water will set the stains.

Mud

Mud should be carefully scraped off washable articles, then you should wash as usual after soaking in pre-wash treatment.

A little cloudy ammonia added to the water is a help for sturdy fabrics (not synthetic or wool).

Scrape solid mud off upholstery and non-washable fabrics carefully, sponge with dishwashing detergent and water. Allow to dry, then spot with dry cleaning fluid.

Paint

Water or acrylic paint stains should be sponged with cold water and dabbed with methylated spirit before laundering or, in the case of non-washable fabrics, carpets or upholstery, sponge with liquid dishwashing detergent.

Sponge oil-based paint stains first with neutral detergent then treat with methylated spirit or turpentine. Test first for colour fastness.

Seek professional help for paint stains if in any doubt.

Rust

Rust stains on enamel baths and sinks can be removed by rubbing with a mixture of salt and lemon juice. Another old remedy is cider vinegar applied with a toothbrush.

To remove rust stains from washable articles, rub with lemon juice and salt and bleach in the sun. Rinse and wash.

Scorch marks

Minor scorch marks on washable fabrics may disappear after simply soaking in cold water. Dabbing with cloudy ammonia before soaking may also help.

Scorch marks can be removed by damping with lemon juice and bleaching in the sun.

Another method is to rub the moistened scorch mark with yellow soap and then bleach in the sun.

Disguise or repair are the only cures for bad burn marks! Try patching, reversing cushions, covering with embroidery or jewellery and, with carpets, patching or covering with furniture. *See* Repairs in chapter 2, 'Cleaning and Brightening' for how to repair a cigarette burn in carpet.

Burns on upholstery can be patched with fabric taken from a part that doesn't show, or covered with cushions.

Soot

Cover soot stains on carpet with salt and then vacuum or dust up.

Sponging

When sponging fabrics to remove stains, change the sponge as soon as you see the stain is moving on to it, otherwise you will transfer it back on to the fabric.

Urine

Thoroughly blot urine stains on carpets and washable upholstery. Then sponge with a solution of bicarbonate of soda and water, white vinegar and water or cloudy ammonia and water.

Washable fabrics should be soaked in cold water, or pre-wash treatment, then washed in the usual way, perhaps with a little ammonia in the washing water.

Vomit

First remove all solids and blot and scrape off as much of the residue as possible. Rinse fabrics that will not be damaged by water with a solution of bicarbonate

of soda and cold water to neutralise the acid, then wash in the normal way. Bad stains may need a pre-wash treatment in an enzyme detergent.

Vomit stains on carpet should be first sponged with bicarbonate of soda and then cleaned with a neutral cleaner (dish-washing liquid) and cold water.

Wine

Sponge wine spills on fabrics or carpet with cold water or, better, soda water or a solution or bicarbonate of soda in water.

Dilute red wine with white before starting treatment.

Washable fabrics can then be laundered or, if any stains remain, soaked in pre-wash treatment.

Salt on fresh red wine stains is a good absorbent. Leave for an hour or two, brush or vacuum off.

Dampen stain and repeat if necessary.

On non-washable fabrics and upholstery, sponge wine spills with cold water. Then cover the spot with salt. Remove after an hour. Repeat if necessary.

HOUSEHOLD STAIN REMOVERS

Bicarbonate of soda *(baking soda)*
Use dry as absorbent, or in solution or paste.

Removes coffee, tea, fruit stains and grease marks. A mild bleach for ivory and silver.

Cloudy ammonia
Use in solution.

Will remove blood, grease and acid stains on hardy fabrics.

Dishwashing liquid *(neutral detergent)*
Use diluted in water. A good mild cleaner for most stains on carpet and upholstery after appropriate pre-treatment.

Eucalyptus oil
Dissolves grease stains and gum residue.

Kerosene
Cleans stove tops and baths.

Polishes taps.

Removes tar spots from cars and self-adhesive labels.

Lemon juice
(citric acid)
Use diluted in water.

Will bleach rust and mildew stains.

Methylated spirit
(alcohol)
Use with caution.

Removes ink and paint stains.

Polishes laminated surfaces.

Salt *(sodium chloride)*
Use dry as an absorbent or in solution.

Lifts wine and fruit juice stains; use also as a soaker for blood, wine and fruit juice stains.

Soda water
(citric acid, in carbonated water)
A useful quick treatment for most stains, especially wine and grease.

Tea-tree oil
Dissolves gum residue.

White talcum powder
Use dry as an absorbent.

Lifts grease and oil stains.

White vinegar
(acetic acid)
Use diluted in water. Good for beer stains.

Will neutralise milk and grease stains and bleach out rust and mildew.

CLEANING AND BRIGHTENING

Cleaning equipment for your home should include a good vacuum cleaner (discuss the relative merits of upright and cartridge models with a dealer before you invest), a stiff straw broom for corners and edges, a soft broom for hard surfaces, a wet mop or squeegee sponge, dustpan and brush, bucket, toilet brush and a good supply of soft, clean cloths. Old woollen garments are excellent for cleaning wooden surfaces. You may also need a scrubbing brush, pumice stone, steel wool and nylon mesh pads.

Chemical cleaners you may need include an ammonia-based all-purpose cleaner, cream or powder heavy-duty abrasive cleaner, floor polish, furniture polish and silver cleaners. Make sure you have on hand bicarbonate of soda (baking soda), methylated spirit and cloudy ammonia (don't inhale the fumes).

When you are working around the house, keep all your cleaning gear together in a plastic bucket, basket or small trolley for convenience.

Never start your cleaning with the kitchen and bathroom — you'll have to use these rooms as a base from which to clean the rest of the house, so leave them until last.

Bathrooms

Never mix chemical bathroom or toilet cleaners. The result could be toxic.

Enamel baths are best cleaned with an ammonia-based cleaner. See chapter 1, on 'Common Stains' for how to tackle stubborn marks.

Do not use harsh abrasives on enamel as it chips and scratches easily.

Bathroom fixtures will come up shiny if cleaned with a cloth dipped in paraffin.

Fibreglass baths should not be rubbed with abrasive cleaners. Use a nylon mesh pad to remove stubborn stains.

Soap film can be removed with fine steel wool.

A small quantity of laundry bleach in the bowl will clean and disinfect toilets.

It will also remove rust stains.

Leave for an hour or two before flushing.

Use approved toilet cleaners only in septic systems.

Clean shower recess tiles with an ammonia-based bathroom cleaner, or use a paste of bicarbonate of soda and water.

Carpet care

Animal hairs are easily removed from furniture or carpets with a damp cellulose sponge or piece of sponge rubber. Rub gently in a circular motion.

Another trick is to wind adhesive tape around your hand or a pad and lift the hairs with the sticky surface. This is a good way to brush clothes, too.

Carpet which has been crushed by heavy furniture can be brought up by a warm iron over a damp cloth. Don't press too hard.

Never scrub carpets. You'll ruin the pile.

Soil retardants, which can be applied to new or old carpet, help carpet to resist damage from accidental spills.

Snip all loose threads in carpet with scissors level with the pile. Never pull loose threads as you might unravel part of the carpet.

When you are shampooing your own carpet, place small pieces of heavy duty plastic under the legs of heavy furniture to avoid them marking the carpet when it is wet. Always vacuum before shampooing.

Always test carpet shampoo on an inconspicuous part of the

carpet before you do the main job by blotting the shampoo on with a white cloth; if any dye comes out, it is best to leave the shampooing to professionals.

Protect your carpet in heavy-duty areas such as inside front or back doors with extra carpet squares or scatter rugs which can be removed and cleaned.

Strategically placed rugs will also keep dust and dirt from landing on the carpet.

Sheepskin rugs can be cleaned with carpet cleaning powder.

Brush it evenly over the rug, roll up and leave for a few hours, then vacuum or shake out the powder.

Chrome

Taps and fittings should not be scrubbed with abrasives or steel wool — the chrome covering will quickly be removed. Use ammonia-based detergent on a soft cloth.

Curtains

Curtains will slide easily if you wax the curtain rods before hanging the curtains. The wax also prevents the rods from rusting.

Boil rusty curtain rings or hooks in vinegar and water for a few minutes to brighten them up.

After washing curtains, hang them while they are still damp as it will be easier to arrange the pleats and folds.

Fireplaces

Always screen open fireplaces to prevent sparks flying and to stop the ash spreading.

Bricks around fireplaces can be cleaned with vinegar.

Floors

A few drops of vinegar in the water used to wash kitchen floors will get rid of grease spots, give a lift to vinyl and cork and remove white patches on quarry tiles.

Scuff marks can be removed from most hard floors with a little methylated spirit. On waxed floors, remove scuff marks with dry steel wool.

Never put too much water on your hard floors or leave water lying on them; the surfaces of vinyl, cork and linoleum may come unstuck.

Use a few drops of mild dishwashing liquid in water to clean vinyl, not harsh cleaners that may dry out the floor and cause it to crack.

Wooden floors should be washed with dishwashing

liquid in warm water, then polished with liquid floor polish.

Do not polish under mats as they may slip and cause accidents.

Waxing of floor surfaces will prevent dirt from sticking to surfaces and save wear and tear.

Glass

Remember to rinse glass that has held milk in cold water first — hot water will make the milk stick to the glass.

Soak stubborn stains on glass in a solution of white vinegar and salt water. Shake the mixture in a badly stained decanter: the friction will help remove the stain.

Use damp tissues to pick up broken glass from floors to save cuts.

The remains of a cake of soap can also be used to pick up glass fragments.

Brand stickers on glass can be removed by covering with oil or butter.

Leave the oil on for a few minutes for the sticker to absorb it, then wipe off.

Delicate glassware should not be machine washed.

A towel in the bottom of the sink will help avoid breakages.

Always slide glasses into the hot washing-up water sideways to avoid cracking them.

Don't use soap or detergent to wash beer glasses — the fat in the soap will make the beer go flat. Just rinse, invert and air dry them.

Ivory
Bicarbonate of soda on a damp cloth will brighten yellow piano keys and plastic. Buff up to finish.

Almond oil provides a protective finish and shine for ivory.

Lighting and lamps
Clean chandeliers piece by piece with a mix of warm water, ammonia and a small amount of dishwashing liquid.

Wipe fluorescent lights regularly with a duster.

Plastic lamp shades should be washed with soapy water in a large sink, but make sure to wipe metal parts carefully.

Metals
Be careful when using brass cleaner on furniture handles, as it can take the colour out of wood.

Make a cardboard collar for the handles and put them around the handles before cleaning.

Clean brass items with a half lemon dipped in salt. Bronze items should be cleaned with soap and water. Brighten chrome with a cloth dampened with ammonia.

Mildew
To clean mildewed tiles or grouting, first wipe over with a damp cloth and detergent, then apply neat laundry bleach with an old toothbrush. Be very careful not to spill any bleach. Wash down thoroughly.

Freshen white grouting between tiles with white shoe cleaner. Apply with an old toothbrush.

Soak rubber bath mats and plastic shower curtains in a solution of laundry bleach and water for a couple of hours to remove mildew.

Rinse and machine wash curtains briefly and hang to dry. A little cloudy ammonia in the water will get rid of soap residues.

Nylon shower curtains crush easily so if you machine wash them, do not spin dry.

Remove from the machine while wringing wet and hang them up to drip dry.

Mirrors
A wipe with methylated spirit will prevent bathroom mirrors clogging up with steam.

Alternatively, rub with soap and then polish with a clean cloth.

Polish mirrors with old newspapers. The printers ink in the papers will make the glass shine.

Odours

Sliced lemon, or a tablespoon of vinegar or cloudy ammonia left in a saucer of water overnight will dispel odours in a room.

A cut onion left in a freshly painted room overnight will absorb the smell.

Put a spring of parsley in the pot when cooking cauliflower or cabbage to lessen the odour.

Outdoor furniture

Scrub any rust on metal outdoor furniture with turpentine.

To clean outdoor furniture, scrub with a soft brush and detergent and rinse off.

Pictures

Don't wet the glass covering pictures when you clean them in case moisture seeps in underneath and spoils the art.

Put a little methylated spirit on to the cloth, not directly on to the glass.

The same applies when polishing wooden picture frames. Put your polish on the cloth, not directly on to the frame.

Do not use furniture polish on gilt frames. Rub with a soft cloth and a little plain flour.

Mildew stains should be removed by an expert.

Place mats
Cork place mats are easily cleaned with pumice stone in cold water. Rinse under cold running water.

Refrigerators
Never leave a refrigerator door shut when it is switched off or mould will quickly form on the inside.

Defrost refrigerators and freezers regularly.

Wipe your refrigerator out regularly with a solution of bicarbonate of soda or white vinegar and water to get rid of odours and to prevent mildew.

Ammonia and cold water is a good cleaner for refrigerator exteriors.

If you're going away for an extended period, clean out the refrigerator, leave the door open and turn the power off if possible.

Repairs
Cigarette burns or other damage on plastic-coated or vinyl flooring can be disguised by a dab of shoe colour dye in the same shade.

A small cigarette burn on your carpet can be easily

repaired. Carefully cut away the burned fibres and from a different spot in an out-of-the-way area cut a small bunch of new fibres without making an obvious hole. Glue into place over the burn mark and cover until set.

Use white nail varnish to touch up chipped enamel surfaces, white woodwork and laminated surfaces.

Shower recesses

Clean shower recess tiles with an ammonia-based bathroom cleaner. For bad stains try a paste of bicarbonate of soda and water.

Clogged shower heads can be soaked in vinegar to loosen mineral deposits and the holes then cleaned with a pin.

A little white vinegar on a damp cloth adds sparkle to glass shower doors and mirrors.

Silverware

A weak solution of bicarbonate of soda (one level tablespoon to two litres of water) will brighten crystal glassware and silver cutlery. Wipe the solution on to fragile articles.

Most silver is safe in the dishwasher, but never machine wash bone, ivory or mother-of-pearl handled cutlery or it will discolour.

If bone handles become discoloured, bleach with lemon juice and water, or a paste of carbonate of soda and water.

Use a good silver polish, or a paste of bicarbonate of soda and water, to clean your silver.

An old toothbrush is useful to get into the crevices.

Keep your silverware in its original velvet or felt-lined boxes to avoid tarnishing and sprinkle with talcum powder or wrap it in acid-free tissue paper away from the air.

A silver-polishing cloth is a useful touch-up tool.

Remember salt, egg and vinegar will stain silver cutlery. Never leave salt in silver containers for long periods as permanent damage may result.

Sinks

Never pour fat down the kitchen sink. Keep a dripping bowl handy for the fat from grilling and roasting.

Keep a rubber plunger as part of your kitchen equipment. If your sink blocks up, first try the plunger after pouring a little boiling water down the outlet.

Cooking salt (a tablespoon or so) in the outlet may also help, or a little cloudy ammonia (don't inhale the fumes), followed by boiling water.

Remember commercial drain cleaning products are caustic and highly dangerous. Avoid spilling on skin or clothes and keep out of reach of children.

A wipe with methylated spirit will keep stainless steel sinks shiny.

Stoves
Wipe up spills on ovens and stove hobs before they harden.

Follow the manufacturer's instructions on oven cleaning. Continuous clean ovens only need a wipe over with a damp cloth, but you should protect the base of the oven with a sheet of foil to catch heavy spillage.

With non-self-cleaning ovens, cleaning is easier if the night before you clean, you leave a saucer of cloudy ammonia in the oven above a pan of boiling water. The ammonia fumes will soften the grease.

Bicarbonate of soda in water makes a good oven cleaner. Pre-heat the oven, turn off, then wipe out with the solution.

Storage
Plasticised hangers with space for soaps and shampoos are obtainable from hardware stores.

Suspend the tidy from the shower arm.

In the laundry, a lockable cupboard for poisonous cleaners is a must when there are young children in the house.

Upholstery

After you have laundered washable loose covers, replace them when slightly damp for a better fit.

Take care when spot-cleaning fitted upholstery.

Always test cleaners first on an area which isn't visible.

Vacuum cleaning

Never let the bag on the vacuum cleaner get too full. This will reduce efficiency and make it harder to empty.

Don't vacuum up pins or sharp objects.

Check the fan-belt fitting regularly in upright vacuum cleaners.

Vacuum flasks

Is the inside of your thermos stained and dingy?

Leave a teaspoon of bicarbonate of soda in boiling water to stand in the flask for a couple of hours to clean and brighten it.

Venetian blinds

An easy way to clean these is in the bath, if you can remove them without too much trouble.

Use dishwashing liquid or a weak solution of cloudy ammonia and water, rinse and rehang in the 'down' position to drain. Leave a towel underneath to catch the drops.

To dust venetians, pull an old pair of woollen or cotton socks over both hands and rub the slats.

Blind tapes can be brightened with white shoe polish applied with a damp sponge.

Vinyl furniture

Clean vinyl with a weak solution of bicarbonate of soda to remove marks, then use a mild solution of washing-up liquid. Never oil vinyl. It is a synthetic material; oil will make it hard.

Wallpaper

Washable wallpaper can be cleaned with a weak warm solution of cloudy ammonia. Use a weak vinegar solution for vinyl papers.

To remove grease stains from non-washable wallpaper, mix a paste of talcum powder and a little water. Allow to dry and remove. Or you could try rubbing stale bread on the wall to absorb the grease.

Windows

Use a proprietary window cleaner, or a weak solution of vinegar in water to clean windows. Only use small amounts of cleaner, as excessive amounts will cause streaking.

Try not to wash windows on sunny days, as they dry very quickly and end up streaky.

Polish with bunches of crumpled newspapers, which won't deposit fluff or lint.

Glycerine rubbed on to windows prevents steam or frost problems.

Wooden furniture

To remove fingermarks and spots from mahogany or polished furniture, first wipe the surface with a weak solution of warm water and vinegar to neutralise the grease, then apply furniture polish and rub till dry. With candle wax, remove any solids first.

Scratches on furniture can be hidden with polish. Beeswax or heavy polish is best for antique furniture that has not been French polished to a high finish.

Liquid shoe polish in a matching colour is another way to disguise scratches on furniture or, for large scratches, fill with plastic wood and touch up with a matching stain.

An equal mixture of turpentine and boiled linseed oil (get this from hardware stores) makes a good scratch treatment for furniture.

Stubborn water rings on polished furniture can be removed with a paste of bicarbonate of soda or table salt and water. After rubbing dry, replace the colour with furniture polish.

Cover small dents in wooden furniture with a wet cloth and some newspaper and iron over the dent until the wood swells back.

Stickers can be removed with a painting of white vinegar. Paper stuck to wood can be removed with salad oil.

IN THE
LAUNDRY

Always follow the manufacturer's directions when using your washing machine. Don't overload and never mix whites and coloureds in the same load or heavy fabrics with delicates. Before you load up, check pockets for pens and money or paper, fasten zips and buttons, turn down cuffs. Test any suspect fabrics for colour fastness, and wash separately.

Your laundry should be equipped with the right laundry powder for your machine (remember front-opening machines use powders with less suds), pre-wash soakers such as bicarbonate of soda or commercial laundry pre-treatments, a laundry bleach and cloudy ammonia for heavy-duty stains. Commercially available wool wash for hand-washing woollens and delicates is a must. If you have a clothes dryer, make sure it is ventilated according to the manufacturer's instructions, and remember to clean the lint filter regularly.

Ironing is an easier chore these days with the advent of steam irons and spray-on starches. Fold-down ironing boards are wonderful space savers; otherwise a portable ironing board that folds away easily is a must.

A steel mesh top on the board means the steam from your iron can escape. You'll need a well fitting ironing board cover with foam or felt underlay, and an iron stand.

Clothes dryers

Don't overload your dryer — read the manufacturer's instructions carefully. If you overload, you'll get wrinkled clothes and the machine will take more time to do the work.

Never put one large article (like a washable bedspread or doona) in the machine that will cause it to become unbalanced. Balance the load with another large article, like a heavy towel.

Always shake wet articles out before loading into the dryer, and when drying is finished, unload immediately to avoid wrinkling.

Colours

Avoid suspect colours running by rinsing them before you wash in cold water to which you have added a couple of tablespoons of salt.

Restore colour to faded black garments by adding a cup of black coffee or tea to the final rinse or you could add half a cup of vinegar if the fabric is suitable.

Jeans, corduroys and dark colours should always be washed inside out to keep their colour.

Cottons
A crushed aspirin tablet added to soaking water will remove perspiration stains and odour.

Soaking in a solution of bicarbonate of soda (a heaped tablespoon to a cup of water) will also do the trick, or a spray of pre-wash treatment.

Spray collars and cuffs of shirts to remove grime before washing. An old-fashioned remedy for ingrained dirt is to scrub with chalk and leave overnight before washing.

Remember, when you wash, any tear or imperfection will be made worse. Do your minor repairs before laundering.

Delicates
Fragile garments can be machine washed on a delicate cycle in warm water if you enclose them in a pillowcase.

Small articles are also best washed in a bag.

Doonas
Always close the zip on doona covers after you remove them for the wash and turn inside out.

To replace a doona cover after it is dry, put your hands up inside the reversed cover, take hold of the top corners of the doona and pull them through the cover as far as possible.

Shake the rest of the cover down over the doona and re-zip.

Doona inserts of synthetic fibre can be lightly machine washed.

Dry inserts in the clothes dryer on medium heat or over two parallel lines on the clothesline.

Shake the filling every now and then during drying to prevent it matting.

Dyeing
Read the manufacturer's instructions before you start and always test dyes on a small piece of fabric first.

Make sure you circulate the dye water thoroughly through the fabric to get an even colour.

Fluff
Fluff can be eliminated by adding 1 cup of white vinegar to the final rinse cycle.

Dark clothes should be washed inside out.

Hair brushes
Wash your hair brushes in a solution of cloudy ammonia and water to

remove the grease. Rinse well. Protect the backs of the brushes from the ammonia as it leaves a film.

Hand washing

Make sure washing powder is completely dissolved when you hand wash or you may get spots on garments.

Hanging

Hang washing out as soon as possible. Dark colours may run if wet washing is left for any length of time in the washing basket.

Turn T-shirts inside out to dry and hang over the line about halfway or less from the top. Peg about two centimetres in from the edge. The peg marks will iron out and the shirts will keep their shape.

T-shirts and cotton jumpers can be dried on discarded pantihose. Thread the legs of the hose through the arms of the garment, and peg the hose to the line. No peg marks to iron out!

A portable plasticised folding clothesline is a great asset — you can stand it in the bath to dry clothes in bad weather or if your outside drying facilities are restricted. You can move it around the home easily for drying or airing.

Always hang drip dry and no iron garments up wringing wet. The wetter the material, the fewer the wrinkles.

Cotton handkerchiefs and table napkins needn't be ironed if you flatten them wet on a tiled bathroom wall.

Steps to outdoor clotheslines can be dangerous when carrying full washing baskets, so avoid them if possible.

Ironing

Make sure your steam iron has reached its set temperature before you iron. Otherwise it may drip on garments.

Irons with frayed cords should never be used.

To keep it smooth, clean the plate of your iron occasionally with bicarbonate of soda on a damp cloth. An old-fashioned remedy is to rub with beeswax, then polish.

Burned-on matter can be removed from the plate with a solution of white vinegar and salt in water.

Standing on an old cushion helps to minimise fatigue during long ironing bouts!

Always move the ironed surface away from you to avoid putting more creases in the fabric.

Never leave water in a steam iron when you have finished for the day — deposits may form that can stain clothes when next you iron.

Never iron velvet directly. Crush marks on velvet can be removed by hanging the garment in a steam-filled shower or bathroom. This works for silk and suede too.

Iron woollens over a damp cloth and gently push into shape.

Warm iron silk garments damp and inside out.

You can make ironing silk shirts easier by putting them in a plastic bag in the refrigerator or freezer for an hour or so before ironing. This works for jeans too.

Always start your ironing with delicates on low heat and work up to cottons needing higher temperatures.

To iron sleeves without leaving creases, place a rolled up towel inside the sleeves.

Put sheets straight back on beds after drying to save unnecessary ironing. Most sheets now contain a percentage of synthetic fabric, so ironing is an unnecessary labour.

If you return sheets to the cupboard after laundering, make sure you put them to the bottom of the pile so that all your sheets wear equally.

Embroidery or articles with raised surfaces should be ironed face down on a towel to allow the pattern to stand out.

To remove the crease mark after letting down a hem, press a hot iron over a vinegar-dipped cloth on the mark until the crease disappears.

Don't iron over sharp objects that can scratch or damage the face of the iron.

When ironing collars, start at the peaks and iron towards the centre back to avoid creasing.

Pleats will always have that just-pressed look if you use a skirt hanger to grip the bottom of the pleats when the skirt is in the cupboard. Lie the skirt on the bed and make sure the pleats are neatly in place before you clip on the skirt hanger.

Leather care

Always stuff shoes with newspaper when they get wet. This will keep their shape.

Never dry leather shoes in front of direct heat. Prop them up or hang them from the rungs of a chair or portable clothesline so that the air can circulate around them.

Try a few drops of vinegar on a damp sponge to remove water marks from leather shoes.

Sprinkle grease spots on leather with talcum powder and leave for an hour. Oil and grease can also be removed from leather by dabbing with eucalyptus oil.

Never store leather bags or shoes in plastic bags. They must be able to breathe or mildew will form.

Make sure you nourish your leather shoes by treating them regularly with a good leather polish and conditioner. Apply a weatherproofing treatment to new shoes before wearing.

Spots can be removed from suede by gently rubbing with an emery board.

Restore the nap to suede by holding the article above a steaming bath or kettle and brushing gently.

Nylon
Yellowed nylon can be rejuvenated by soaking overnight in a weak solution of bicarbonate of soda before laundering.

Nylons and synthetics can be machine washed at low temperatures on the delicate cycle; make sure you hang them up wet to drip dry to avoid wrinkling.

Raincoats
Never put plastic or rubber raincoats in the clothes dryer. Air dry only.

Silk
Silk should be washed gently as wool in cool water. Dry away from direct sunlight.

Slippers
Foam carpet shampoo will clean soft slippers well. Use a damp sponge.

Synthetics
Synthetics should be rinsed in cold water last — this reduces wrinkling when drying.

Tennis shoes
Canvas tennis shoes can be machine washed. Put them in the machine with a couple of old towels.

Washing machines
Never use more detergent than is recommended, as it will only be wasted and you could damage your washing machine.

Stand washing machines on hard surfaces on lino squares to prevent them travelling when they are in operation.

Woollens
Never use bleaches, ammonia or pre-wash treatment on wool.

Use a good wool wash and dry garments flat on a towel (squeeze excess out gently in a towel first).

Do not expose wool to direct sunlight or heat.

Iron woollens under a damp cloth and gently push into shape.

Work clothes

Cloudy ammonia added to the washing water will help to remove mud, grease and bloodstains on work clothes.

HOME
MAINTENANCE

If you know how to carry out simple repair jobs around the house, you'll save a fortune in trades bills. These days most of the larger hardware stores have staff qualified to help with advice on how to tackle maintenance problems and what materials you need. Your basic equipment should include a stepladder, at least one strong hammer, pliers, a small hacksaw, screwdrivers of various sizes and including a Phillips head, chisel, adjustable wrench or spanner, fuse wire, glue, screws and nails and a good tape measure (a three-metre steel tape should be adequate). You'll build up a store of such items as picture nails and wire, strong adhesive tape, sandpaper and perhaps a hand drill as you need them. And if you wish to advance to more ambitious projects, you may need to acquire power tools and a stronger power drill.

Do not attempt any electrical or plumbing repairs that could jeopardise your safety.

Changing tap washers

Don't try to replace washers yourself on the modern mixer type of tap.

To change a washer on a conventional tap you will need a spanner or wrench, a new washer or valve assembly, and pliers.

Consult staff at your hardware store on the type of washer needed. You may need to take the old washer or valve assembly to the store.

1 For a cold water tap, turn off the water at the mains tap (usually at the meter).

2 For a hot tap, also turn off the hot water service at the unit and the water supply wheel at the unit.

3 Turn the tap to full 'on' position.

4 Dismantle the tap: first screw off the tap handle and cover, using your hand or a wrench padded with a cloth. Then unscrew the nut at the base of the top section of the tap. Take off the top section. Be careful to lay out the pieces of tap so that you can identify them for reassembly!

5 Lift out the valve assembly from inside the base of the tap with pliers.

6 Replace the washer or the entire valve assembly.

7 Reassemble the tap and tighten the nut at the bottom of the top section.

8 Turn the water on at the mains and at the hot water unit and turn it on, or relight the unit if your water is heated by gas.

9 Make sure the tap you have repaired is turned off!

Cleaning a blocked sink

To clear a blocked sink outlet, you will need a bucket, wrench or spanner and a one-metre long piece of sturdy wire to clean out the cause of the blockage.

1 First try to clear the blockage by pouring a little boiling water down the sink, followed by a handful of salt, or a tablespoon of cloudy ammonia and then a little more boiling water.

2 If the sink is still blocked, place a bucket under the U pipe.

3 Undo the cap at the bottom of the U pipe using wrench or spanner. (Some modern sinks don't have this opening. Instead you will have to unscrew the nut on the S bend nearest the sink, then the nut nearest the floor or wall to remove the whole S bend pipe.)

4 Clear the blockage with a piece of wire.

5 Flush out the pipe with water.

6 Replace the screw.
7 Replace the cap, or S pipe and screw in. Be careful if caustic soda or drain cleaner has been poured down the sink in an effort to clear the blockage. These substances are toxic.

Drawers

Sticking drawers can be quickly fixed with soap or candle wax, or even a little oil on the rails, after a light sandpapering.

Stop drawers sliding all the way out by fixing a small block of wood either on the inside back of the drawer or inside the front of the drawer opening as a stopper.

Electrical cords

Worn cords on any electrical appliance should be replaced professionally.

Gutters

Check gutters and downpipes regularly for blockages. Use the garden hose to flush them out and pinpoint trouble spots.

Hammer and nails

To prevent wood splitting when hammering in nails, blunt the point of the nail a little.

Another trick is to push the nail into a cake of soap to make it easier to hammer in.

A fibreglass handle on your hammer rather than a wooden one reduces shock and fatigue to the hand.

When using a nail punch, make sure you hold it absolutely straight.

A thin piece of wood slipped under the claw head of a hammer will protect surfaces from damage when you are pulling out nails.

It will give more leverage too.

Use the right nail for the job. Bullet heads are for beneath wooden surfaces, flat heads will not pull through timber; and clout-type nails are usually galvanised for metal finishes. Get advice from your hardware store on which type of nail you need.

Hand drills

Hold your drill steadily and straight up and down.

To remove the drill from the hole, don't reverse the action. Keep drilling but lift the drill gently up at the same time.

Ladders

Never mount a ladder unless it is securely fixed in position. And never place extension ladders more than a quarter of their extended length from the wall.

Keep your tools in a safe place when working on roofs and ladders.

A bag attached to a hook on the ladder or to a belt around your waist is a good idea.

Never lean a ladder against guttering, it could bend the guttering out of shape.

Leaking and noisy cisterns

If your cistern is overflowing, you may be able to deal with the problem yourself with the aid of pliers and a screwdriver.

Lift off the cistern top and check the floating ball attached to the inlet valve by a lever.

This lever shuts off the inlet valve when the water in the cistern reaches a certain level.

Is the ball too high in the tank? Try gently bending the arm a little.

Is the ball waterlogged? If so, you will need a new one.

Is the ball in the right position? Bend the arm gently towards the centre of the tank.

An overflowing cistern can also be due to a worn rubber washer on the outlet valve mechanism at the bottom of the tank.

If this is the case you will need to replace it.

1 Turn off the supply of water at the tap at the base of the toilet.
2 Empty the tank by flushing the toilet.
3 Remove the pin that attaches the float arm to the valve assembly.
4 Unscrew the cap on the valve case and remove the piston and the worn washer.
5 Replace the washer, then reassemble.
6 Turn on the water and fill the tank.

Light globes

Never change a globe when the light is switched on.

Follow the maker's instructions carefully when changing a fluorescent tube. If a tube is flickering, first check that the metal pins at the end of it are not bent or dirty before you buy an expensive new tube. Also, check that the starter part is not faulty by swapping it with a starter from another light. If this is the problem, you can buy a replacement starter.

Mending chairs

Here's how to fix wobbly chair legs.

1 Turn the chair upside down and remove the leg if you can without damaging it. Hot vinegar will sometimes dissolve furniture glue.
2 Sand away the old glue and replace with fresh wood glue.

3 If the leg is still too loose in its socket, pad the end out with a piece of old stocking.
4 Coat this with glue, replace the leg and cut off any visible edges of stocking.
5 If you can't remove the chair leg, use the nozzle of the glue tube to trickle glue into the socket around the leg.
6 Leave upside down to dry.

Mending fuses

Do not attempt repairs of any electrical appliances yourself. If an appliance does not function after you have been through the simple checklist provided by the manufacturer, **seek professional help.**

To replace a fuse, you will need replacement fuse wire, a blade screwdriver and possibly a torch if your fusebox is in a dark corner.

1 **Switch off the power supply at the main switchboard.** If this is not clearly marked, seek professional help.
2 Once the power supply is off, pull out and examine each fuse plug in turn to find the faulty one. You will see burn marks and the fuse wire will be broken.
3 Loosen the screws holding the wire in place (do not remove the screws), take out the broken wire, and replace it with a length

of fuse wire cut to the same length and of suitable weight (15 or higher amp fuse wire is for power and appliances, 8 amp for lights).

4   Twist the wire around the screw at one end, pass it through the hole in the fuse wedge and wind it around the screw at the other end.

5   Tighten the screws but don't stretch the wire tight. The wire should be around the screws in the turning direction.

6   Turn on the power and test the fuse with your face turned away in case the fuse is still faulty.

7   Get professional help if it is.

Roofs and spouting

Check roofs and spouting regularly for leaks and blockages, but don't attempt to do this unless you feel confident. Seek professional help if in doubt.

Screwdrivers

For maximum efficiency the screwdriver should exactly fit the head of the screw you are working. If it is too wide it will come into contact with the surrounding materials and perhaps damage the surface; if too narrow it may damage the screw head.

Remember when tightening and loosening screws: to

the right is tight and to the left is loose.

To loosen stubborn screws and nuts, wipe with a little white vinegar or penetrating oil and allow it to soak in.

Nail polish is a useful fixative for screws and bolts that constantly work loose.

The longer the screwdriver, the better the leverage.

Silicone sealers

Use silicone caulking compound in tubes to repair and replace damaged mortar between baths and walls in bathrooms and to seal kitchen sinks. Your hardware store will advise

you of the right type of sealer for the job.

1 Make sure the area to be sealed is as smooth as possible and the crumbling old grouting has been scraped out and removed. Wipe the surface to be sealed with methylated spirit or turpentine.

2 Use masking tape to cover the edges of baths, tiles, sinks and so on, so that excess sealer does not ooze on to surfaces.

3 If you are sealing edges along a bath or sink, fill it with water so that the gap to be sealed is at maximum size.

4 Seal steadily along the gap with the nozzle of

the tube, smoothing up to the edge of the masking tape with a spatula.

5 Remove the masking tape before the sealer dries to avoid pulling it out.

6 Clean up any excess sealer.

Consult your hardware store for advice on sealers and glues for windows, gutters and roofs.

Before using any adhesive, make sure surfaces are dry and free of dust and grit.

Squeaking hinges

Try rubbing dry soap on squeaking hinges.

Another way to stop hinges and floorboards squeaking is to sprinkle talcum powder on the hinge or between the cracks.

Tape measures

Never force your tape measure in or out. If stuck, make sure that the release is working.

Don't bend your tape measure sharply as it may cause a permanent kink.

Always measure twice for the quantities of materials required for any job — it could save you money.

Learn the span of your own hand spread out — little finger to thumb. It's a useful rough measure.

Tiles

Replacing a tile or two is
easy when you know how.
You will need adhesive,
grout, a toothed spreader
and something flexible,
such as a piece of leather.

1 Scrape or scrub the
   area, then leave until
   damp but not wet.
2 Clean the tile
   thoroughly.
3 Apply wet adhesive
   with the toothed
   spreader, which
   should scratch along
   the surface and leave
   trails of adhesive.
4 To place the new tile,
   put adhesive around the
   edge in a continuous
   line to prevent gaps
   between old and new
   work.

5 Press the new tile into
   place, making sure the
   spacing is even.
6 When setting is
   advanced, use a damp
   cloth to get rid of
   excess adhesive.

Wait at least 4 hours before
grouting. Mix the powder
with water to a soft, toothpaste consistency and push
it fully into the cracks. Pull
away any excess with a
flexible tool, fully exposing
the edges and corners. As
the surface dries, use dry
grout powder on a soft
cloth to polish the area.

Ventilation

Make sure you check fans
and vents in your skirting
boards, walls and ceilings
regularly and ensure they
are not clogged.

PAINTING AND DECORATING

Most simple painting jobs can be tackled by the home handyperson. Staff at hardware stores and paint shops will give advice on procedures and what you need to buy but for even the most basic painting task you will need several grades of sandpaper (and preferably, a block to fix it on), a scraper and sugar soap to clean surfaces, a filling compound, a chemical stripper in some instances (poison — use with great caution), or a hot air stripper, turpentine, brushes, undercoat or primer and the preferred type of paint — water, acrylic or oil-based.

With the advent of pre-pasted wallpaper, hanging is an easier job. You'll need an accurate measure and a plumb line, a trough or baby's bath to soak pre-pasted paper, or a paste bucket and adhesive for normal paper, a table to cut paper on, a sponge for smoothing out the paper on the wall, a metal straight-edge ruler, a trim knife and scissors.

Bathrooms

When renovating bathrooms keep the following points in mind.

1 Adequate ventilation. Steam needs an outlet. Consider a ceiling fan.

2 Adequate light. Be sure to install a light over a makeup mirror. Brighten up dark bathrooms by installing a skylight.

3 Don't have switches near water, or where children can reach them with wet hands.

4 If you are installing a new bath, make sure the new frame is adequately waterproofed.

5 Flooring should be water resistant and easy to clean.

An easy way to give your bathroom a new look is to buy new matching taps and fittings, or co-ordinated accessories such as towel rails.

When fitting towel rails, don't forget to hang them high enough so that large towels don't drag on the floor.

Brighten up your old bathroom scales by covering them in adhesive paper to match the walls.

Old porcelain baths can be reglazed. Get advice from your plumber.

Add glamour to your bathroom with an assortment of small soaps and bath salts in a glass or ceramic bowl or wicker basket tied with a bow and set beside the bath or hand basin.

Brush and roller care

When painting, don't overload your brush with paint.

Never leave your brush in the tin of paint or rest your brush on its bristles; it will bend out of shape. Lie it flat.

Clean the brush immediately after finishing — don't leave paint on the brush for more than 30 minutes.

After cleaning, wash the brush in warm soapy water. Hang to dry or lie it flat.

Before you start painting, feather the clean brush up and down against your hand to get rid of any loose bristles that might spoil the job.

When using a roller, don't overload it with paint. When you have finished, roll off excess paint on sheets of newspaper and clean according to the type of paint used either with water or turpentine. Hang your roller up to store it, or stand on its end.

During short breaks from painting, wrap your brush

or roller in plastic film to stop paint hardening.

Children's bedrooms

Vinyl flooring, with washable cotton scatter rugs, is a sensible choice for children's rooms.

In later years, you can carpet the room.

Buy single trunk beds with a trundle bed for visitors, or bunks which give double the accommodation in the same space.

Make sure all fabrics used in furnishing children's rooms are washable and flame resistant.

Curtains and upholstery

Tired of straight curtains? Tie each of your matching cotton curtains in the centre about 30 centimetres from the ground. Then pick up the outside corners and pin higher on the curtain than where they are tied. This gives a pretty butterfly effect.

Use unusual objects such as decorative stars and silk scarves to catch your curtains back.

Using flat cotton sheets for curtains can be an easy and inexpensive way to give a room a new look. Measure the length and width of the area to be covered — you'll need a sheet that is at least double the width of the window for a full curtain. As the sheet is already hemmed, all you need to do is turn it up if it is too long and sew tape and rings to the top. Or just hem and push on to a rod. Use a matching pillowcase to make cushions.

You can also make an upholstered chair look like new with a pretty sheet or a printed ethnic bedspread draped and tucked over it. Gather the front of the arms and catch with bows. Tuck the sheet well down into the back of the chair.

The secret of plump scatter cushions is to make their covers a little too small —

or buy the cushion a little too large for the cover!

Remember for curtains to hang straight they should have a weight sewn inside the hem at the bottom corner.

Austrian balloon blinds are easy to make out of panels of lace the same size as your window. Sew white plastic rings in parallel lines down the panels about 25 centimetres apart.

Tie white nylon cord to the bottom ring in each row and run it up to the top. Make a casing for a rod at the top and thread the curtain on to the rod and fix at the top of the window. Fix metal screw eyes at the top of the window to line up with the plastic rings and run the cords between the eyes and along to one side of the window. Knot the cords together to form a pull.

Furnishing ideas

Attractive tables can be made out of stools, birdbaths, barrels and cases by simply topping them with glass cut to fit.

Framed photographs or prints look attractive on small tables or shelves combined with posies of simple flowers or a bowl of a single variety of fruit.

Folding screens are cheap to buy and easily made to look glamorous. Paint, or drape with an attractive or unusual scarf or length of fabric.

Kitchens

When planning or renovating your kitchen, try to avoid through traffic to the back garden or to another room via the main kitchen area.

Plan the available workspace carefully. There should be plenty of bench room near the stove — and the bench should have a heatproof finish on it.

You should allow serving space on the bench area as well as a food preparation area.

Place the refrigerator at the far end of the kitchen cupboards and nearest the exit. Once food has been removed from it, the cook won't need access but others might.

Make sure kitchens have plenty of light, a pleasant outlook and good ventilation. A good fan is essential.

In a narrow kitchen, consider finger pull catches on cupboards.

Moving furniture

Before moving heavy furniture or appliances over vinyl or wooden floors, slip a piece of old blanket underneath to avoid marks.

Painting ideas

A small room can look bigger if it is painted white or off-white.

Use paint imaginatively on old furniture, picture frames or mirrors.

Wooden floors can transform a room if they are painted in a high gloss finish.

Painting inside

Thorough preparation is the secret of a good paint job if you want a professional finish.

Old wallpaper may have to be removed, flaky old paint sanded down and holes caulked to a smooth surface. Use an undercoat after washing the walls down with sugar soap.

When painting a room, first remove the furniture, or cover it with a dropsheet. Cover the carpets and floor with dropsheets.

Paint the ceiling first. Use a roller for large areas and finish around window frames, light fittings, switches and doors with a brush.

Protect edges of door and window frames with masking tape or with a smear of petroleum jelly.

When painting a ceiling, tie a discarded nylon sock around the brush above the handle and paint will not drip down onto your hand.

Enclose light fittings in large plastic rubbish bags to protect them from drips. Use smaller bags to cover doorknobs that can't be taken off.

Remove all possible fittings such as handles from surfaces to be painted before you start. It's much easier than painting around them.

If ceilings are mildewed, first wash it off, then apply a coat of size or anti-mould preparation (a gelatinous or glutinous preparation available from hardware stores).

When painting skirting boards, hold the carpet back with a stiff piece of cardboard or ply. Use masking tape on floorboards to protect your brush from dust.

Leave a bowl of water with a sliced onion or lemon in it overnight to get rid of the paint smell.

Don't paint windows shut. Slide them up and down after you have painted them and leave them slightly open to dry.

Always take drawers out of the cupboard frame to paint them. Stand the drawer face up and leave to dry this way to prevent drips.

Painting outside

Never try to paint surfaces that are wet. You must wait for dry conditions, but if the sun is too hot it may cause the paint to wrinkle.

If you are using a ladder, make sure it is securely fixed.

New timber surfaces should be primed and sanded and any holes caulked before paint is applied. New brick should be dusted down and undercoated.

Old surfaces should be cleaned, sanded and old peeling paint scraped off and made smooth before primer or undercoat is applied.

Prune shrubs and growth back from outside paint work to avoid spoiling.

Painting tips

Don't use a screwdriver to prise lids off paint tins. It will spoil the edge of the lid and make sealing difficult. Use a broad bladed knife instead and prise up evenly around the edge.

When hammering the lids back on, cover with a cloth to prevent splatters.

Paper plates make good stands for paint tins to catch drips.

Remember to record details of the paint you use on the lid or bottom of the tin: the maker's name, the colour, where used in the house, any special mixing details. This will make matching or reordering easy.

Store paint tins upside down. This will prevent a skin forming on the surface of the paint. Make sure you fix the lid on securely.

Water-based paints and acrylics are the easiest to use and clean up. Oil-based paints will give a higher gloss — but the higher the gloss, the more imperfections will show through.

Sanding

When hiring or buying a sanding machine to sand down weatherboard floors, choose one with a dust collector.

When hand-sanding timber finishes to stain, sand with the grain and wipe with a turpentine rag to finish.

After hand-sanding walls and before you paint, remember to wipe down surfaces and get rid of any dust.

Wallpapering

Always buy extra paper in case you need to patch or match later.

You will need extra with patterned wallpaper if the design needs matching.

A mixture of hot water and methylated spirit will usually take off old wallpaper that won't come off with water.

Paint the mixture on and leave for 20 minutes or so, but keep the wall damp.

Don't forget that stencils can add an interesting finish to a striped wallpaper or a plain-finished room.

When you are repairing a damaged spot, tear the edges of the patch rather than cutting them.

This will give a less visible finish on the wall.

Prepare your walls carefully before hanging wallpaper.

Sand and wash painted surfaces, fill holes and seal if necessary. Old paper should be removed unless it is a perfect surface and the paper design won't show through.

Hang paper so it overlaps doors and windows, then cut around the frames with your trim knife. Don't try to measure wallpaper to fit first.

A clean paint roller on a handle is a useful tool to smooth out wallpaper. Alternatively, use a firm sponge or squeegee.

SEWING AND KNITTING

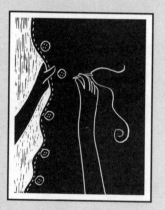

SEWING AND KNITTING

Whether or not you intend to take up serious dress-making, every householder needs some basic sewing equipment to carry out simple sewing repairs and maintenance jobs which can be costly if you have them done professionally. These include sewing on buttons, repairing small tears, altering hems and replacing elastic and cords in pyjamas and pants. You should have a good pair of scissors, a selection of cotton and silk threads, needles and pins, spare shirt and trouser buttons and a tape measure.

Knitting is a relaxing and creative hobby and the variety of patterns and instruction books on the market make it easy to learn so we have included a few hints for knitters here.

Buttons

Push a pin into the fabric where a button is to go and sew over it as you put the button on. When you remove the pin, the button will be easier to fasten as it won't sit too close to the fabric. Or you can lie a matchstick on the fabric and sew over it.

When the button is on, wind your thread around several times between the button and the fabric to form a 'shank' which will give extra strength.

Buttons can pop off heavy coats due to strain. Try threading the buttons on to hat elastic first, then sew this on to the garment.

Sew buttons on heavy fabrics with a double thread for extra strength. Don't use this technique on delicate fabrics such as silk or very fine cotton where the double thread might tear.

Strengthen machine-made buttonholes with a little clear nail varnish at the back.

When sewing on four-hole buttons, sew and finish each set of holes with a separate thread. This will give an extra 'life' to the buttons.

Paint loose threads on buttons with nail polish if you can't repair them straight away.

Equipment

An easy way to sharpen your scissors is by cutting through sandpaper.

Push pins and needles (carefully!) through your hair to make them shine. The oil in your hair will make them easier to push into stiff fabric.

A small magnet is handy to pick up dropped pins. Keep one in your sewing basket.

A shoebox makes a useful storage unit for sewing patterns if you stack them vertically.

Keep a small magnifying glass with your sewing equipment to help you thread needles.

Hand sewing

Name tapes should be hand sewn down the rib of knitted garments, not across, so that the ribbing can move evenly when washed and the tape won't be seen from the outside.

When choosing thread for your sewing jobs, always buy thread that is a shade darker than your fabric. Thread always looks lighter when it is sewn than on the spool.

Draw your thread through beeswax to avoid tangles and strengthen the thread.

To avoid tangles, never have your thread too long — 45 centimetres is a good length.

Stiff fabrics such as denim can be more easily sewn if held together with clothes pegs.

Hats
Hat too big? Glue a strip of foam rubber inside the headband for a snug fit.

Hems
When finishing the hem on a new garment, always let it hang for a day or two with the hem unfinished to allow the fabric to settle.

If possible, get a friend to mark the hem for you when it is your own garment. Remember to wear the correct shoes.

If you have to pin up your own hem, do it this way:

with the skirt on, stand against a table and put a row of pins at hip level, rotating around and using the table as a measure.

Then take the garment off, and measure down the skirt from the pins to the required length. Insert a new row of pins to get an even hemline.

Press an unfinished hem with the marking pins in place before you sew it. Press it on the wrong side with a piece of paper between the layers of fabric to avoid a mark on the right side.

When hand-finishing a hem with slipstitch, remember to catch only one thread of the fabric at a time to ensure maximum invisibility.

If you are left with an ugly mark after letting down a hem, rub it with a weak solution of white vinegar and water. Place a cloth over the hem and iron dry.

Another way to disguise a hem mark is with braid or ruffles.

For a temporary dropped hem repair, use adhesive tape to stick it up.

Knitting

If you can't knit it is very easy to learn on some small, simple garment like a woolly hat or a scarf. By the time you've one or two such items you'll be able to tackle a jumper. Find an instruction book in the library that is aimed at beginners and has patterns star-rated according to difficulty.

Keep tension even when knitting and never stop for a break in the middle of a row.

When learning knitting techniques, use larger sized needles and bulky wool.

Be careful not to split your wool with the point of the needles.

When working one plain, one purl, remember to switch the wool from back to front as you change stitch.

Keep balls of wool in a plastic container and feed the yarn through a small hole in the lid to prevent tangles when knitting.

If you find you knit purl stitches more loosely than plain, hold your wool tighter on purl rows.

Or if this doesn't work, you could even use slightly smaller size needles for purl rows.

Keep both front and sleeve pieces of a cardigan even by knitting them at the same time and on one set of needles. You will be able to maintain a constant gauge.

When knitting a patchwork quilt, don't cast off when you have finished a square. Just change colour and knit on till you have the length of patchwork you require.

This means time saved in sewing up the finished article as you just join the strips.

Never join a new skein of wool in the middle of a row.

If you can't find a helper to hold skeins of wool taut for you while you wind them into balls, use the back of an upright chair.

Always tuck a moth-protector into your balls of wool before storing. Use strongly scented wrapped soaps or sachets of Epsom salts.

To get the kinks out of wool that has been unravelled, wind it around a filled hot water bottle and leave for a couple of hours. The heat will release the kinks.

Never hang heavy woollen garments. They will drop and sag. Store flat between tissue paper layers.

Knitting — decreasing

Always try to decrease on the plain side of your work rather than the purl.

If you are using the knit-two-stitches together

method, and you are knitting in plain, the decrease stitches will slant to the right. If you are knitting in purl, they will slant to the left.

Knitting — increasing

If you are picking up a loop to increase stitches, you must twist the loop as you place it on your left needle, otherwise you'll get a hole in your work.

Knitting mistakes

You can pick up dropped stitches using a crochet hook.

When you are replacing work on your needles after correcting a mistake, make sure you have the stitches facing the right way.

The needles should go through the back of the stitch for the knit side, the front of the stitch for the purl side.

Knitting needles
Choose needles that are a different colour from your wool.

Plastic needles are light and quiet, but easily broken. Metal needles last, but can split your wool. If you use wooden needles, keep them smooth with sandpaper.

Knitting wool
Always buy pure wool yarns rather than synthetics. Wool is more

expensive, but bargains can be found in sales or discount outlets. Wool also requires more careful washing, but the greater warmth, softness and comfort that only wool can give makes the effort well worthwhile.

Make sure you buy enough wool from the same dye lot to complete your project. Dye lots can vary.

If you are forced to use wool from different dye lots, use a ball from each lot and knit row and row about. Any colour difference won't be noticed.

If your wool is very soft or slippery, try knitting in a strand of cotton thread to keep the work from stretching out of shape.

Old, handknitted jumpers can be unravelled and the yard reused to knit something smaller. Wind it into skeins, using the back of a chair, and tie each one.

Then wash the wool carefully to remove some of the kinks; this will make it easier to handle.

Machine sewing

Chiffon, georgette and other sheer fabrics can be a problem to machine sew. Try stitching them together with thin white or tissue paper underneath to stop them puckering up — it can be removed quite easily after sewing.

If you have trouble machine sewing in a straight line, lie a strip of masking tape on the material as a guide. It can be easily removed.

Adhesive tape stuck on the wrong side of the fabric will prevent fraying when you are making button-holes.

Remove the tape after you have made the buttonhole.

Mending

If buttons rip off and leave a hole in the fabric underneath, patch the hole with a piece of tape or fabric remnant then sew the replacement button on to this.

Use a safety pin or bodkin to pull elastic or tape through the casing around the top of pyjamas or knickers.

Attach the elastic securely and don't forget to fix it to the fabric at the end where you start in case you pull it right through and have to start all over again.

Here's a quick way to do invisible mending of small tears. Turn the garment inside out and cover the tear with white of egg.

Press a piece of material of the same colour on to the tear (on the wrong side) and make sure the torn edges meet neatly over it. Iron the makeshift patch

on — the egg white will act as an adhesive.

To darn a patch, first stretch the hole over a support such as an old light globe or darning 'egg' and make a row of stitches around the edges of the hole to neaten it. Then take your thread from side to side across the hole, catching it at the sides. To finish, work the other way, across the hole, weaving in and out of the first lot of threads to form a patch.

Do not knot wool or thread when darning — this could make bulk to catch, or walk on in the case of socks. Begin and end your work with three or four small stitches on top of each other.

Holes can be darned, or patched, or patched from underneath and mended neatly using the patch as a base.

Sewing ideas

Make great nightshirts and short nighties out of discarded men's shirts.

Cut off collars and sleeves if desired, and pretty up with braid or lace.

Men's business shirts make wonderfully voluminous smocks for young art students or, with the collars removed, Indian-style shirts for teenagers.

Cut off old jeans or cotton trousers at the knee to recycle them into fashionable shorts.

With skill and ingenuity jeans can be converted into spunky denim miniskirts. Cut them off just above the knee, remembering to include a narrow hem allowance. At the centre back, make a vent or insert a kick pleat using fabric taken from the lower legs.

A full length slip is easily converted into a half slip by cutting off and inserting elastic at the waist.

Patchwork should always be made with the same type of fabric and should be colourfast if you intend to wash it.

Use silk thread for silk material, cotton thread for cotton patchwork. In any case, have the article dry cleaned for the first clean and, of course, dry clean only with silk.

Sew knee patches on children's trousers **before** they get torn.

Stitches

Use slipstitch to finish hems and cuffs. Bring your needle through the fold of the hem, then pick up one or two stitches on the skirt. Then go back to the hem fold about 5 centimetres further on.

If you finish the hem edge by machine, you can simply catch the hem edge on to the skirt fabric using a diagonal stitch.

Zippers

When replacing a broken zipper, make sure you iron the seam allowances neatly so you can replace the new zipper in exactly the right position.

Zippers can be put in by hand. Use small, neat backstitching.

FIRST AID

Your medicine cupboard should be kept locked at all times. It should be high up out of the reach of small children.

Keep it stocked with basic first-aid equipment including adhesive dressings of various sizes and shapes, crepe bandages, cotton wool, gauze dressings, antiseptic lotion or ointment, pain-relieving tablets (aspirin or paracetamol), a thermometer, medicine glass and eye bath, splinter forceps and scissors, and an itch-relieving cream or lotion such as calamine lotion.

It is most important to keep a good first-aid manual in your medicine cupboard or kitchen drawer. The authorised manual of the Australian Red Cross Society is a good standby. But whatever handbook you buy, make sure it shows you how to carry out emergency first-aid procedures such as mouth-to-mouth resuscitation and heart massage. Every adult in your household should be familiar with these procedures. They could save a life if carried out correctly.

Write in the manual your doctor's phone number and emergency ambulance and hospital numbers, together with the number of the nearest poisons information centre.

Seek medical attention for any severe symptoms or injury — persistent pain or headaches, fevers, heavy bleeding — or if you suspect poisoning.

Bites and stings

The bites and stings of insects and sea creatures can be serious. In Australia, for example, the stings of the box jellyfish and bluebottle jellyfish and the bites of the redback and funnel-web spiders can lead to great pain, swelling, difficulty in breathing, symptoms of shock, unconsciousness and even death in the case of the spider bites. The poisonous tentacles of the blue-ringed octopus are also deadly.

Act quickly and follow the specific emergency procedures in your first-aid manual if you suspect anyone has been stung or bitten.

Try to obtain a description of the animal or insect so that the correct anti-venom treatment can be given.

All snake bites should be treated as a serious emergency.

Keep the victim still and cover the area of the bite with a firm bandage.

If the bite is on a limb, use a piece of wood as a splint to immobilise the area. Seek medical attention immediately and follow the emergency first-aid procedure for snake bite in your manual.

Try to obtain a description of the snake so that the right anti-venom treatment can be given.

Even minor insect stings can occasionally provoke allergic reactions similar to the ones described above.

Watch victims carefully after bee and wasp stings. Get medical advice if adverse reactions occur, and follow the emergency first-aid procedures for bites and stings in your manual.

Eucalyptus oil or tea tree oil dabbed on the spot will take the pain out of minor insect stings.

If you don't have any calamine lotion, the itch of a mosquito bite can be relieved by rubbing with a piece of raw onion.

A paste of bicarbonate of soda and water applied to insect stings and bites is another old remedy for pain and itching.

The itching of sandfly and tick bites can also be relieved by dabbing with white vinegar.

Never squeeze a bee sting out between finger and thumb. This will spread out more poison. Apply an ice pack first, then gently lift or scrape the sting out with a sterilised needle.

Swab the stings of bluebottle and box jellyfish with vinegar to alleviate the pain.

Pour turpentine or kerosene over ticks to remove them. Never squeeze or pull them out.

Bleeding and minor wounds

Make sure you wash your own hands before dealing with any injury where the skin is broken. Clean minor cuts and wounds with cotton wool in cool clean water, then place a piece of sterile cotton wool or gauze over the wound and hold firmly until it stops bleeding.

If the injury is on a finger or limb, hold it above heart level. When bleeding stops, cover the gauze with an extra sterile dressing.

Solutions of either bicarbonate of soda or salt and water are mild antiseptics.

All dirty wounds, even if minor, are susceptible to tetanus infection. Always ask whether an injury happened out of doors. Was it caused by dirty or rusty tools?

Check whether the injured person has been immunised against tetanus. Get medical advice if necessary.

Animal scratches and bites are prone to infection. Check that tetanus immunisation is current and get medical advice on whether further protection is necessary.

Severe bites need stitching and professional dressing; an oral course of medication to prevent infection may be necessary.

When bleeding is severe and the wound is serious, apply a sterile pad and bandage firmly.

Get the victim to medical help quickly or ring an ambulance. Heavy bleeding can kill if not quickly controlled.

Remember a deep wound which seems to be healing can be infected beneath the surface, so get medical advice.

Signs of infection in wounds include soreness, swelling, redness, pus oozing from the wound, fever, swollen glands and red lines leading up the arms and legs.

Blood groups

Always have blood types for yourself and other members of your household noted in your medicine chest or emergency manual.

Breaks and fractures

Breaks and fractures are manifested by pain, swelling and deformity and loss of movement.

Victims may be in shock, so treat accordingly.

Do not give the victim food or drink.

Do not attempt to straighten a suspected fracture. Immobilise the limb, following the emergency first-aid procedure in your manual. Seek immediate medical help.

Bruises, strains and sprains

These results from damaged or stretched ligaments (sprains) or muscles or tendons (strains).

Rest mild sprains and strains, and bandage them firmly with a crepe bandage and without impeding the circulation.

Use ice packs over a two-day period.

If a bruise is on a limb, a firm bandage may help. Ice packs should be applied to bruising, but no heat.

Severe pain from sprains and strains means seek medical help.

Burns

Burns from any chemical substance should be washed immediately and thoroughly under running water so that the dangerous substance is flushed from the skin.

Get medical advice **immediately** for all chemical burns. Find out the substance that has caused the burn so that it can be neutralised.

Minor burns and scalds where the skin is reddened and blistered but **not broken** should be treated immediately — either hold the burn under running water or wrap in loose wet bandages until the pain stops.

Minor burns are often best left to heal in the air. If you do apply a dressing, make sure it is non-adhesive.

Do not apply butter or grease to a burn. This could cause infection and may retard healing.

Do not put anything on or over burns when the skin is broken. Seek medical advice for these burns, as they easily become infected.

Do not pull off clothing or fabric which is stuck to a burn. The skin will peel off. Seek medical advice.

Do not break the blisters which form over burns. The liquid inside the blister is a healing agent.

Choking

Choking is caused by a blockage of the airway or windpipe by a small object. In serious cases, the victim can't breathe or speak.

Unless the object is clearly visible and you can carefully remove it without pushing it further down, seek immediate medical help and follow the emergency first-aid procedures in your manual.

A sharp blow between the shoulder blades may release blockages.

Convalescence

Both adults and children need special attention when recovering from illness or injury. They may become easily tired, irritable and emotional.

Do not allow too many visitors or overstimulating activities during recovery from illness; encourage convalescents to do only as much as they can without exhaustion.

If you have to look after someone over a long period of convalescence, it's a good idea to move them out of the bedroom during the day as soon as they are well enough and if injuries allow it.

Install the patient in the family or living room where they can watch television or rest in a different environment.

This is a good intermediate stage between illness and total recovery.

Help the patient back to the bedroom to rest if there are any signs of exhaustion.

Keep convalescents comfortable by straightening and making the bed as needed. Keep an eye out for any sign of soreness through pressure on hips and back which could lead to bedsores. Sponge the convalescent often if they are not strong enough to shower or wash.

Make sure food is served attractively. Never leave half-eaten food in the room — it is unhygienic and unattractive.

Convalescent cookery

Here are some simple recipes to tempt convalescent or sickroom appetites.

Beef tea. Shred 250 g rump steak finely and place in a jar with a pinch of salt, 250 ml water and 1 teaspoon lemon juice. Stand the jar, with its lid on, in a saucepan of boiling water. Cook gently for 3-4 hours.

Chicken broth. Take 1-2 chicken carcasses and a couple of feet, bring to the boil in a large saucepan of water. Skim and add a chopped onion, salt, pepper, piece of celery, parsley and carrot and a bay leaf. Bring to the boil again and simmer, covered for at least an hour. Cool and strain the stock, skimming off the congealed fat. Return the stock to the heat, add a cup of pearl barley (or rice if preferred) and simmer for half an hour.

This chicken stock can be varied with the addition of vegetables such as celery, or enriched with pieces of diced poached breast of chicken.

Egg flip. Beat 1 egg, 1 teaspoon sugar and 1 teaspoon sugar.

Bring 250 ml milk to the boil, pour over the egg mixture and stir well. Sprinkle with nutmeg and serve in a large drinking glass.

Make your own lemon cordial by dissolving a cup of sugar in 2 cups of boiling water. Allow to cool and add the juice of 3-4 lemons. This cordial should be diluted with cool or iced water to taste.

Fairy cakes. Preheat oven to 200°C/400°F. Cream 1/4 cup of butter with 1/4 cup caster sugar, add a beaten egg, a few drops vanilla essence and 3/4 cup self-raising flour alternately with 1/4 cup milk. Half fill paper patty pans with the mixture and bake for 12-15 minutes.

Fairy cakes can be iced, or the mixture varied with the addition of a few sultanas or grated lemon peel.

Gruel. Boil 250 ml milk. Mix 1 tablespoon oatmeal with 2 tablespoons cold water and pour the boiling milk over the mixture.

Stir for 3 minutes, then strain into a saucepan and cook for 8 minutes. Serve in a cup and saucer with sugar and butter.

Other suggestions for a light diet are junket (if the patient is allowed milk), jelly, vanilla ice cream, stewed or puréed apple, steamed or poached fish or chicken.

Convulsions and seizures

Keep a convulsing person from harm by moving dangerous objects out of the way, but do not try to restrain the person.

Do not attempt to put anything in the mouth of a person having a convulsion.

Check that the person is fully conscious after the convulsion. Seek medical help to establish the cause.

If unconscious or not breathing, follow the emergency first-aid procedures in your manual.

Coughs and colds

Colds are best treated by rest, plenty of fluids and a light diet.

Unless there is a secondary infection (tonsillitis, pneumonia, ear infection) antibiotics will not help. Take aspirin as directed on the packet for fever and a cough mixture if necessary.

Honey and lemon juice in a little warm water makes a good cough mixture.

Gargle with table salt dissolved in warm water to relieve a mild sore throat.

If coughing, sore throat or fever persists, or if earache develops, get medical advice.

Barley water made from boiling strips of lemon peel, a handful of pearl barley and water is a good mild drink for cold and fever sufferers.

A little petroleum jelly carefully applied on a cotton bud to the insides of the nostrils will relieve cracks and dry soreness.

Cramp

Give sips of water to relieve cramp due to heat exhaustion.

Massage the area gently and make sure clothing is loose in the case of muscular cramps.

Croup

Croup usually strikes young children and is an infection of the voice box.

The hoarse cough can be relieved by steam — use an electric frypan of boiling water to make the room moist, or sit in a steamy bathroom.

If the condition gets suddenly worse, seek medical help.

Drowning

Help a person who is drowning from the edge, if you can, by extending something for the victim to hold on to. Hold on to something yourself so that you don't fall in.

If you must enter the water, take something to tow a conscious victim — a towel, for example.

If the victim is unconscious, drag them to shore and follow the emergency first-aid procedure for drowning in your manual.

Ears

Never poke sharp objects into ears. Seek medical attention for all ear problems.

Electric shock

Don't touch the victim of an electric shock until you have switched off the power either at the switch (not if it is wet!) or at the fuse box.

If you can't do this, pull the victim away using a poor conductor of electricity — a wooden pole or rope, but **nothing metal**. Make sure you are standing on a dry surface.

If the victim is unconscious, seek medical help and follow the emergency first-aid procedures for electric shock in your manual.

Epileptic fit *see* Convulsions

Eyes
If you have sand or grit in your eye, try pulling the upper lid over the lower one and moving it gently from side to side.

For a harmful substance, you should flush out the eye with clean water or saline solution (towards the outer side of the face) and seek immediate medical attention.

Do not attempt to remove anything stuck firmly on the eye.

Fainting
People usually recover quickly after fainting.

Seek immediate medical attention if breathing stops.

After recovery, put the patient's feet up.

Head injuries
Victims of head injuries can suffer partial or full loss of

consciousness, headaches, blurred vision, nausea, loss of memory, confusion, weakness, bleeding from the nose and have pupils of uneven size. They may have convulsions.

The effects of head injuries may appear up to two days after an accident.

Do not leave victims of head injuries alone.

Seek immediate medical advice for all head injuries and follow the emergency first-aid procedures in your manual.

Heart attacks

Symptoms of heart attacks include sudden acute pain in the chest which spreads to the arms, jaw and back, dizziness, irregular pulse, sweating, nausea and breathlessness. The victim may collapse. If you suspect an attack, seek immediate medical attention, call an ambulance and follow the first-aid procedures in your manual.

Heat exhaustion

Symptoms of heat exhaustion include nausea, faintness, sweating and breathlessness.

Drink plenty of fluids and rest in a cool place if you are affected by heat.

Loosen clothing and sponge your skin with cool water.

If your feet swell up in the hot weather, bathe them in cool water and rest them in an elevated position. Seek medical attention for severe cases of heat exhaustion and sunburn.

Ice packs

Ice packs can be used to take the sting out of insect bites and to ease the pain of toothache.

Never apply ice directly to the skin, wrap it in a cloth.

Use an ice pack on sprains, bumps and bruises.

Patent ice packs filled with chemical like those used by sports coaches are useful to keep in your freezer.

These are pliable so you can bend them around the injury. They can also be boiled and used as hot packs.

Medication

If your doctor prescribes a course of medication, always finish the whole course even if you feel better before the end. Otherwise the illness may recur.

Nosebleeds

Pinch the nostrils and lean the victim over a sink until bleeding stops.

If the bleeding persists, get medical advice.

A cold cloth on the forehead may help.

Poisons

Symptoms of poisoning include vomiting, diarrhoea, convulsions, weakness, breathing difficulties, unconsciousness, burns in and around the mouth, and symptoms of shock.

If you suspect poisoning, seek immediate medical help and follow the emergency procedures in your manual.

If the victim is conscious, try to establish what the poison is and how much has been taken. Keep the victim calm.

If carrying out emergency resuscitation procedure, be careful to wipe around the victim's face and mouth to avoid contact with any dangerous substance.

Pulse

The pulse is the pumping action of the heart felt in waves along the arteries.

It is useful to know whether a pulse is strong, weak or irregular as this can indicate an illness or abnormality.

Measure the pulse at the wrist, on the thumb side of the forearm bone, where the artery runs beside the bone and just above the crease in the wrist.

1   Use your fingers to take the pulse, not your thumb as it has its own pulse.

2 Use a watch with a second hand.

3 Count the number of pulse beats per minute. An average adult rate is 72 beats per minute. However, this can vary under stress, or when taking exercise or alcohol. It can be as low as 60 and as high as 80.

Young children have a faster pulse rate, and very fit people usually have a slower one.

Shock

Shock may result from a physical accident or fall or an emotional cause. In cases of mild shock, the victim feels ill, dizzy, weak and cold and has a rapid, irregular pulse.

Victims may also yawn and sigh frequently. See that the victim lies down with legs up and is kept warm and comforted. Loosen tight clothing. Seek medical help.

Do not give food or drink to shock victims as it may cause vomiting.

If a shock victim is unconscious, seek immediate medical help and follow the emergency first-aid procedures in your manual.

Stomach pain

This can be caused by anything from gastro-enteritis or appendicitis to simple indigestion.

If you are unsure of the cause of the pain and what treatment to apply, give no food and seek medical help.

If stomach pain is accompanied by other symptoms such as high temperature, diarrhoea and vomiting, seek immediate medical help and follow the appropriate emergency first-aid procedures in your manual.

Sunburn

Prevention of sunburn is better than cure. Always wear a hat, sunblock and protective clothing in the sun.

Remember that sunburn is not just caused by exposure to hot sun; it can also occur in hazy conditions or be caused indirectly by reflection from water, sand and snow.

If you must get a tan, limit your exposure to the sun. Start with about 15 minutes exposure per day and gradually increase the time to about 30 minutes until you begin to tan.

Cold teabags or tea itself used as a poultice can ease sunburn, or add teabags to a warm bath.

You can also swab yourself with a cloth dampened with vinegar to relieve sunburn.

Unconsciousness

Unconsciousness may result from brain damage (e.g. head injury or stroke); loss of blood; lack of oxygen in the blood (e.g. drowning) chemical changes in the blood; or overdose of certain drugs.

Seek immediate medical help for an unconscious victim and follow the emergency first-aid procedures in your manual.

Unconscious patients should not be left unattended in case they stop breathing.

HOUSEHOLD
PESTS

Prevention is better than cure, so follow a few simple rules to discourage common pests such as flies, moths and mosquitoes from entering your home.

Never leave food uncovered or scraps on kitchen benches overnight. Clear away dirty dishes as soon as a meal is over. Make sure you have insect screens on all exterior windows and doors. Close any opening that mice and cockroaches could squeeze through. Seal the bottom of doors with rubber strips. Keep your garbage bins disinfected and away from the house. Brush spider webs as soon as you notice them.

Minor infestations of common household pests can often be dealt with by using old-fashioned remedies rather than relying on pesticides.

Borax is a good standby to use as a bait, and lavender oil, eucalyptus oil and citronella oil (available from chemists) are strong deterrents and useful items to have on your shelves, as insects dislike their strong smell. Dried or fresh herbs have many uses as insect-repellents.

If the old remedies don't work, you may have to

choose a good insecticide or get professional pest control experts. Remember to keep any poisons in high lockable cupboards, well out of the reach of children and pets.

Ants

Don't tempt ants inside. Discourage them from your home by keeping sweet and greasy foods in well-sealed cupboards.

Follow ants back to their nest and destroy it with boiling water or insecticide.

Deter ants by making a talcum powder barrier across their tracks. Ants dislike walking across the powder.

Bay leaves scattered in cupboards is another simple way to discourage ants.

Ants also dislike lavender. Sprinkle a few drops of lavender oil at their point of entry into your house to keep them away.

Homemade lavender oil is easily prepared by soaking lavender heads in good-quality olive oil for a few days. Strain the oil and bottle.

Remember that ants come into the house in dry weather. Keeping your garden well watered is one way to keep them outside.

Borax powder mixed with sugar or flour makes a good ant bait. Sprinkle this outside where the ants are entering the house.

Peppermint essence is an old-fashioned ant bait. Sprinkle it at their point of entry or around the nest if you can find it.

Argentine ants

Argentine ants are reddish-brown in colour, slightly smaller than small black ants and do not smell when squashed.

They are attracted to food scraps and food smells on unwashed dishes. They even find their way to discarded clothing.

Argentine ants have to be tackled by pest control experts because they seem to resist the usual deterrents.

Cockroaches

Cockroaches can slip through very narrow spaces. Seal all possible points of entry thoroughly. Use the appropriate sealant for gaps in wooden floors.

Use a bait of equal portions of borax powder and sugar to combat cockroaches. Leave it where you have seen them emerging. Pyrethrum powder is an effective alternative

Cockroaches are deterred by vanilla pods and cucumber peel. Scatter these throughout food cupboards.

Fleas

Animal fleas are the most common; they live on blood and give an unpleasant bite. Human fleas that carry plague and typhus are rare in most Western countries.

However, animal fleas can live on human beings, and infest carpets, beds and upholstery.

Vacuum frequently and thoroughly to avoid fleas in the home. Scatter lavender oil through the house. Keep a few sprigs of lavender in cupboards and tucked under carpets.

Remember that fleas can live a long time without food.

Warmth stimulates them. You can suffer a flea plague in a house that has been unoccupied for some months.

If you do suffer from a flea plague, vacuum thoroughly and dispose of the contents of the bag carefully, by burning if necessary.

Remember you must get rid of the flea eggs as well as the fleas themselves. Keep your animals free from fleas. Inspect them frequently.

Animals can be allergic to flea bites and this can lead to serious skin problems such as eczema.

Dust your pet with derris dust, or comb lavender or eucalyptus oil through the coat.

Bath pets in a mild shampoo with a few drops of eucalyptus or lavender oil added.

To avoid reinfestation from unhatched flea eggs, wash your pet's bedding and sprinkle with derris dust or lavender oil, or destroy the bedding altogether.

Check and treat any other areas your pet inhabits.

Fresh mint leaves scattered on and under pet bedding is an old remedy for fleas.

Flies
Keep your home flyproof by installing screens on windows and outside doors.

Wrap up garbage and keep bins securely covered.

Remember to block the bottom of your chimney off with fly wire in summer to stop flies entering.

Any of the lavender, eucalyptus and citronella oils will repel flies.

Smear or dab a little on face and hands.

Old-fashioned sticky flypapers are an effective way to trap flies. Make your own with honey smeared on fine sandpaper.

Lavender planted around the house is a more attractive fly deterrent.

Fly killer

Mix ½ teaspoon black pepper, 1 teaspoon brown sugar and 1 teaspoon cream, and leave the mixture in a saucer in the kitchen.

Fly repellent

Rub doors and windows with a cloth soaked in either oil of lavender; water in which onions have been boiled; or ammonia. This will keep flies out of your home.

Fly swatter

A plastic fly swatter is a worthwhile purchase; it is an easy way to get rid of occasional insects that come inside even if you have screens on your windows. Big blow flies, mosquitoes and other large insects are easy targets.

Insect spray

You can very easily make your own insect spray by following this recipe.

Crush 100 g garlic and pour 2 teaspoons paraffin oil over it. Cover the mixture and allow to stand for 48 hours. Then make a pure soap solution, say

30 g soap powder in 500 ml hot water. Pour it over the garlic mixture and mix them together. Allow to stand for 24 hours, then warm slightly, strain and bottle.

Remember to label the bottle.

Use 1 part in 100 parts water.

Mice

Avoid mouse infestation by having well-fitting window screens and sealed floors that can't be chewed through.

Stop mouse holes with steel wool and remember that mice can squeeze through tiny openings.

Peppermint essence sprinkled around points of entry or on pieces of cloth or paper left in likely haunts may deter mice.

Keep all food in sealed cupboards.

Traps are the most effective remedy if your mouse problem is confined to a small area — and small numbers.

Bacon is a favourite food of mice. Use the rinds and grease to bait traps.

Outside, keep garden compost in containers, and try to avoid too many food scraps in your compost mix.

Mosquitoes

Stagnant water is a breeding ground for mosquitoes. Make sure your fishpond is stocked with fish or frogs that eat mosquito larvae.

Frequently change the water in pools and bird baths and in your pet's water bowl.

Supplement your insect screens and wire doors with mosquito nets in the bedroom if you are in mosquito territory.

Oils of lavender and citronella are good mosquito repellents. Dab on, and use citronella and lavender candles to keep mosquitoes at bay when you are outside at night.

Moths

Most modern carpets are moth-proofed. However, to destroy moth eggs in old carpets, iron the carpet over a damp cloth. The heat and steam will destroy the eggs.

Clothes and carpet moths, like most insect pests, dislike strong smells.

Keep sachets scented strongly with dried lavender, cinnamon and cloves in your cupboards to keep the moths at bay.

Cotton lavender (santolina) is another good moth repellent. Grow it in your garden and use the leaves in sachets or scatter in drawers. Naphthalene, camphor and turpentine will deter moths.

Store your woollens in plastic bags with lavender sachets.

Always make sure clothes and fabrics are clean before you put them away.

Moths are attracted to food, perspiration and other stains.

Camphor is a tried and tested remedy against clothes and carpet moths.

Soften the pungent odour by combining camphor

with dried lavender in sachets in cupboards or under carpets.

In the kitchen, try to keep all foodstuffs in covered containers to avoid contamination by food moths, weevils and mealworms.

A cup or small jar of used cooking oil is a good bait for food moths, which will drown in the oil.

Replace the bait as often as needed and have one on each shelf where food is stored.

Food moths are repelled by bay leaves. Scatter them in your kitchen cupboards.

Possums

Possums can be a problem even in the suburbs.

They have to be dealt with by a professional pest controller, who will trap them and release them away from urban settlement.

Rats

Rats live in roofs and outhouses, or in shrubs and trees around houses.

Discourage infestation by blocking off any possible entry points into your home or into your roof under the eaves.

Don't keep food in outside sheds unless it is in vermin-proof containers.

Check gutterings and spoutings regularly for any sign of rat infestation such as droppings.

Make sure your insect screens fit tightly.

If you suspect there are rats in or near your home, get professional help to eradicate them. Do not attempt to deal with the problem yourself. Rats can be aggressive when cornered.

Weevils

Tape some bay leaves to the lid ..of a food container to get rid of weevils.

To make them leave stores of dried fruit, add a piece of lemon rind to the jar.

CHILDREN

CHILDREN

If you have children, you must arrange the household so that they can live and grow happily in a safe environment. Plan your home to minimise risks for children and anxiety for yourself. Remember that children need to be able to explore to develop. A few basic precautions will make this process relatively accident-free.

In this chapter, you will find tips on how to make your home a safe place for children. There are also suggestions on using children's equipment, how to make meal times happy times and keeping children occupied on rainy days.

Children around the house

Tuck up the edges of overhanging tablecloths. Better still, do away with these while young children are in the house. Use place mats instead.

Beware of leaving plastic bags near babies and young children. They can cause suffocation if pulled over heads and noses.

Keep pets and pets' feeding utensils away from young children and do not leave animals alone with them.

The helplessness of babies and young children and the sounds they make can arouse aggressive instincts in animals.

Keep staircases fenced off with a barrier that can be removed by adults when necessary.

Never leave objects or appliances on the stairs for you to trip over when you are carrying a child.

Make sure glass doors and tables are made from laminated or toughened glass.

Teach children at a young age to go down stairs on their bottoms or to slither down backwards.

Don't leave handbags lying around, as a toddler will gleefully eat the contents.

Make sure electrical switches are covered and earthed — you can get childproof caps at hardware stores to cover switches.

Keep matches, lighters and cigarettes out of the reach of children.

Make sure all open fires, radiators and other heating appliances are securely guarded. If possible, use heaters with thermostats that switch off if the heater is upended.

Children in the bathroom

Never leave a baby or young child alone in the bath — even for a minute. If you have to answer the door or the phone, take the child with you.

Always put the cold water in first and then add the hot when bathing children and babies and turn the hot water tap off first, to avoid scalding.

Test the temperature first with your elbow or the inside of your wrist.

Keep medicines and bathroom cleaners out of reach high up in a locked cupboard. Make sure all medicines are clearly labelled.

If you need to bathe a baby and you don't have a small bath, use a plastic clothes basket and sit it in the big bath. The baby will feel more secure.

Use as little water as possible in the bath.

Never leave a baby alone on a changing table or bed. Babies are great rollers.

Never leave electrical appliances near the bath, because of the danger of electrocution.

Children's bedrooms

Keep furniture safe in children's rooms. A shallow step will make it easier for a young child to climb into bed.

Avoid sharp corners on furniture.

Electric blankets shouldn't be used on children's beds, as they can overheat quickly. Use doonas instead.

Make sure windows have secure wire screens which cannot be pushed out. Open windows from the top so children cannot get out.

Don't have pillows in a baby's cot. Babies can suffocate easily.

Make sure the bars on the cot are not so far apart so that the baby's head could get stuck.

Keep baby cots away from windows, as they could choke on blind cords.

Sleep your baby on his or her back or side, not face down.

Dress children in fire-resistant sleepwear.

Children in the kitchen

Keep all cleaning chemicals and substances that could be harmful if swallowed out of reach in high, securely fastened cupboards.

If possible, keep children out of the kitchen when cooking; use child fences across doorways.

Keep the handles of pots and pans on the stove turned to the back so that children cannot pull them over and burn themselves.

Keep curtains well away from the stove area.

Keep electrical appliances at the back of shelves and disconnected. Don't let appliance cords hang down so that children can pull them.

Lockable refrigerators are a good idea, or else secure then with a piece of elastic shock cord.

Never leave your baby propped up with a bottle. The baby could choke.

For the same reason, never leave young children alone when they are eating.

Keep cups of tea, coffee and soup away from children as they may reach for your cup and spill it over themselves.

Children outside

Beware of water! This applies to garden ponds and swimming pools. Make sure these are fenced off — it only takes a minute for a child to drown.

Keep toddlers away from barbecue areas for as long as the barbecue is hot.

Make sure you have a secure front fence and high latch on the gate to stop your children getting into the street.

For security and safety, do not let children play in the street unless closely supervised.

Even very small children on tricycles should wear a helmet.

Make sure workshops are locked, dangerous substances are out of reach and power tools are unplugged.

Never leave a child in a parked car, not even for two minutes.

Protect babies and children from the sun. Make sure they wear shady, wide-brimmed hats, long loose clothing and 15+ sunblock.

Make sure there are no poisonous plants in the garden.

Babies and children easily get dehydrated in hot weather. Give frequent cool drinks of water and insist on rest times to avoid exhaustion.

When crossing roads, don't allow the pram to protrude over the gutter while waiting.

Children's toys
Choose safe toys for your children. Remember that most toys will be well chewed and sucked by young children, so make sure they don't have harmful knobs and buttons that could be swallowed.

Always buy toys that are suited to your child's age.

Check that the finish on painted toys doesn't contain lead.

Buy toys that are easily cleaned.

Equipment
Keep a harness permanently in the high chair to prevent swan dives.

Bouncinettes should be kept on floor level, as if they are left on benches they can be bounced off.

Be aware that baby walkers allow extended mobility and reach, enabling a child to reach power points, electrical equipment, televisions and so on.

They also tip over easily when going from carpet to lino and vice versa or if they run into dropped articles.

Equipment that hangs from doorways and permits a child to jump is not suitable for infants.

Stability in prams is important for the safety of children. If the wheels are too small, then the pram may tip over.

Feeding
Place a plastic tablecloth or newspaper under the high chair to minimise cleaning up after mealtimes.

Save time by preparing large quantities of puréed vegetables and storing them in ice cube containers in the freezer for later use.

Make your own teething rusks by cutting wholemeal bread into sticks and baking in a very slow oven for about an hour.

Make food fun by varying colour and texture, making food look appealing (cut bread into fun shapes), using garnishings (such as cheese, raisins and fingers of fruit) and varying the venue. On hot days, eat outside on a blanket on the lawn.

High chairs that can be converted to a chair and

table as your child grows may be a worthwhile investment.

Rainy day activities

Blow up balloons, then let them go to see whose goes the furthest. Or attach a piece of string between two chairs and have a game of balloon tennis.

Use empty plastic bottles as skittles and try to bowl them over with a light ball or a potato.

Make a cone out of cardboard and attach a ping pong ball with string, then try to catch the ball in the cone.

Give each child a torch and tell them to direct the beam on to the ceiling of a darkened room. One of the spots of light is 'it' and has to try and catch the others.

Using old Christmas or birthday cards, make holes along the outline of the objects in the picture.

Use long shoelaces to sew round the outlines.

Hide and seek is a great old favourite rainy day activity.

Another is to make tents or cubby houses by throwing sheets and blankets over the furniture.

Have a secret selection of colouring and puzzle books

tucked away in a wet afternoon box.

Story books come in handy, especially if children are unwell.

Strangers

Children are not able to distinguish potential child molesters from harmless strangers; indeed, child molesters can be charming.

Teach your child these simple rules:

1 Stay at least two arms' lengths from any stranger.

2 Do not talk to strangers even if they know your name.

3 Do not take anything from a stranger, even if it is something that belongs to you.

4 Do not ever go with a stranger, even if the stranger says that he or she was sent by a parent or teacher to collect you.

PETS

Pets need the appropriate surroundings for their happiness and comfort. Choose a pet that will fit in with your home and lifestyle. Don't choose a large dog if you live in a flat! Make plenty of inquiries about characteristics of breeds and types of animals before you make your final decision.

The amount of difference an active, strong-willed pet will make to your household is only one step below that of a child. If you intend owning a pet, then it is a good idea to get acquainted with a reputable vet.

Children and pets are not always compatible. However, as children grow, the responsibility of owning and caring for a pet can be an important part of their development.

Basic necessities

Be prepared to spend money on the equipment and medications necessary to keep your pet in good condition, happy and contented.

Dogs need a kennel outside, a basket or blanket inside, a collar and lead or choker and chain and feeding bowls and a brush and comb.

Cats need their own basket (preferably in a high spot, such as on a wide shelf or couch), collar, feeding bowls, brush and comb and a litter tray if they are to be flat dwellers.

Fish will need a tank, air pump, water filter, thermometer and perhaps a heater for tropical fish, as well as sand, pebbles and plants for the tank.

The water in the tank should be changed frequently to avoid pollution.

Never change the water in a fish tank all at once. Replace about a third every fortnight, so that the correct temperature and acidity is maintained.

Birds will need a good-sized cage inside with accessories such as swings and perches — unless you plan to build a proper aviary in the back garden. An indoor cage should be out of draughts and away from kitchen fumes.

Remember, birds like a blanket over their cage at night.

Be prepared to take care over your pet's health. Check with your vet on the necessary inoculations.

For example, dogs must be inoculated against distemper, parvovirus and hepatitis when they are puppies; kittens should be inoculated against feline enteritis and cat flu. Boosters are necessary every year.

You must exercise dogs regularly; the distance walked and amount of

exercise depends on the size of the dog.

Dogs and cats need regular worming. Discuss this with your vet.

Remember, smaller dogs usually live longer than large ones.

Care in hot weather

Dogs and cats usually eat less in hot weather.

Make sure your pet has a cool shady area in which to shelter in hot weather.

Be vigilant in grooming pets in hot weather. Fleas tend to proliferate in warm conditions.

Never leave pets in a car with the windows completely shut — even when the weather is quite mild. Animals and birds get dehydrated very quickly.

Desexing

This operation will not adversely affect the health and personality of your pet. Desexed animals do not get fat because of desexing — they get fat because they are being overfed and underexercised!

In most areas, registration fees are less for desexed animals.

Desexing will mean that animals are far less likely to roam. Males are less aggressive and females do not come on heat and are therefore less trouble to look after.

Diet

Dogs and cats need plenty of water to drink. Make sure your pet always has a bowl of clean water available.

Discuss your pet's diet with your vet. All animals have special requirements. An all-meat diet is not satisfactory for dogs and cats — nor is a completely vegetarian diet.

Feed your pet at regular times every day.

If you are changing your pet's diet, introduce new

foods gradually or it may get diarrhoea.

As they get older, dogs and cats often need less protein. Supplement their feeds with carbohydrates such as boiled rice, mashed potato or pasta.

Don't forget dogs need to use their teeth to keep them clean — a large bone every week or so is a good idea.

Don't give small bones that can splinter — like a chicken or chop bone. These may stick in the dog's throat.

Cats can develop teeth and gum problems too, if fed exclusively on a 'soft' diet. Encourage your cat to eat

some dried food, or chew on a flat bone occasionally.

Birds need shellgrit in their diet to aid digestion and calcium such as a piece of cuttlefish to condition their beaks.

Birds need a lot of water so get them a spill-proof demand water supply for drinking and a shallow dish for bathing.

Don't overfeed fish! Feed them small amounts once or twice a day but remove uneaten food from the tank after five or ten minutes.

Don't encourage animals at the table while you and your family are eating. Pets get fat if fed extra goodies outside mealtimes and will quickly develop a begging habit if encouraged.

Health and cleanliness

Keep dogs and cats free from fleas. Inspect them regularly, at least once a week. Flea bites can set up an allergic reaction which can lead to serious skin problems.

As a deterrent, dust your animal with derris dust, or comb lavender oil through their coats.

(Make your own lavender oil by soaking lavender flower heads in olive or almond oil for a few days. Strain and bottle.)

Wash your dog in a baby's bath or in the back garden. Use warm water and a mild shampoo with a few drops of eucalyptus or lavender oil.

Salt water should always be washed off dogs' coats after a swim. The salt can irritate the skin.

Bush or stable fly bites can cause dogs great distress and can lead to infection. Dab citronella oil on your dog's ears and tail to ward off these pests.

Groom long-haired cats regularly — and short-haired breeds if they enjoy it. Normally, there's no need to bath cats as they keep themselves clean.

Make sure you keep covers on children's sandpits to prevent cats soiling them.

Medication

Use a syringe or eye dropper to give dogs and cats liquid medication orally.

Your vet will show you how to give tablets to animals.

Stand your dog on a mat in the bath to administer medication. Spillages won't matter and it's easier to handle the animals in the confined space.

Ticks

If you live in a tick-prone area, inspect your pet regularly for ticks. Tick poison causes paralysis and death to animals. Ticks are about the size of a pea. Look for them all over your animal, and in the ears and mouth.

Cut ticks off, but do not put any chemicals on the sting. These may cause a further, possible fatal dose of poison to be released into the animal's system. Take your pet to the vet for treatment.

Training

A clock in the basket of your new puppy or kitten will help it to get over separation from the mother and strange surroundings. Wrap the clock in a woolly jumper or blanket. The ticking of the clock sounds like the mother's heartbeat and will reassure the animal.

Cover your fireplace opening when you bring a new kitten home. If your new pet is frightened, it might disappear up the chimney.

Remember puppies like to chew and pull trailing objects. Don't leave cords dangling from electrical appliances or tablecloth corners trailing.

Provide puppies with their own playthings, such as an old shoe or a rubber bone.

Provide a scratching post for your cat. You can easily make one from a solid piece of wood covered with a piece of old carpet of textured fabric. Attach this to a wall so that it doesn't fall on your pet. If you can train your cat to use it, this will save your own upholstery from damage.

Keep your cat's litter tray clean or it will go elsewhere!

Mothballs placed on furniture will keep cats off. And orange peel scattered in gardens will also repel cats.

To start house training, put your puppy or kitten on a newspaper or dirt tray after every meal and at night. Give lots of positive encouragement if the animal uses the spot. If and when mistakes are made, show the animal and scold, but do not rub its nose in it — in animal terms, this is a sign of encouragement!

Be lavish in praise when the animal goes in the right spot.

Gradually move the tray outside, continue to take the animal after meals and remember to reward either with affection or praise every time the puppy or kitten performs in the right place.

The secret of all animal training is to reward

immediately and **consistently** so that behaviour patterns are reinforced.

Train your pet to answer to its name by using this technique.

Remember the reward (or punishment) for an animal must immediately follow the act — otherwise the animal will not understand.

Dogs should be taught to 'sit', 'heel' and 'stay' for their own safety as well as the convenience of their owners.

You should never allow your dog to pull on the lead. A choker chain used correctly will soon control

this irritating and
dangerous habit.

It is preferable for one
person to train a dog — if
other family members are
to take part in the training,
make sure they use exactly
the same commands and
techniques or the animal
will be confused.

Use short one-word
commands.

Bell your cat to stop it
killing birds. You should
also keep it in at night.
Make sure the collar you
use is not too loose so that
it snags on something.
Attach reflector tapes
to it.

MORE
GENERAL
HINTS

MORE GENERAL HINTS

In this section you will find tips on security and safety in the home, storage, moving house and plant and car care, as well as some ideas on the extra touches that make your home a special and individual place: entertaining, formal dining and the serving of wine. Use these suggestions as starting points for these enjoyable and rewarding activities.

A small herb garden can be grown even on an apartment balcony without too much trouble, so we have also suggested a few ways in which herbs can be used in beauty care and natural health remedies.

Avoiding accidents — electrical

Never use electrical appliances with worn insulation.

Seek professional help to repair them.

Never operate a switch with one hand and touch a metal tap or water with the other.

Metal and water are both good conductors of electricity.

Never handle hair dryers, radios or other electrical appliances near water or leave them where they might fall in.

Don't try to mend electrical equipment yourself. Seek professional help.

Avoiding accidents — fire

Never start fires with inflammable liquids, or throw inflammable liquids on to fires. The fire can backtrack via the liquid to the container and the person holding it.

Never store petrol in the house or in a warm place. It is highly inflammable.

Never use water to put out an electrical, fat or oil fire. Smother the flames with sand, a lid or a blanket.

Never air clothes near an open fire which can give off

sparks, or too close to any other heater, where there could be a danger of them catching alight. Remember children or pets can push or knock airing garments into the danger zone near a heat source.

Avoiding accidents — inside and outside

Don't leave cupboard doors or drawers open where they could cause bumps and cuts.

Never leave things lying about in dimly lit areas where people could stumble over them.

Never leave garden tools or hoses where people could trip over them.

Don't leave piles of garden rubbish lying around which could contain thorns or spines and be a breeding ground for insects, spiders and mice.

To avoid falls, always clean up grease and oil immediately when it is spilled on the kitchen floor; likewise soap and shampoo in the bathroom.

Never climb up on a ladder that is not fixed securely in position, or on a wobbly or fragile chair, stool or box.

Beauty
Here's a simple homemade face mask for acne sufferers. Mix rolled oats with lemon juice and leave overnight. In the morning

add a teaspoon of beaten egg and some honey to form a thick paste. Thin out with cucumber juice if necessary.

Apply to your face and leave for 20 minutes, then gently sponge off.

Cold tea makes an excellent astringent or skin refreshener. Also use cold tea bags or pads to relieve tired and sore eyes.

Petroleum jelly is an efficient way to remove face and eye makeup — and quite inexpensive. It nourishes the skin also.

Infusions of rosemary (for brunettes) and chamomile (for blondes) make hair

shiny if used as a final rinse after washing.

Garden soil won't get under your nails if you lightly scratch a moist cake of soap before starting your weeding.

Car care

The most common cause of hard starting is dirty or worn spark plugs. Plugs are easily cleaned, but the gap should also be checked with a gauge. Alternatively, you could simply buy a new set and replace the old ones. They are easy to remove when the car is hot.

To prepare your car for sale, pay careful attention to cleaning and polishing.

A damaged number plate can spoil the whole effect. Touch it up with hobby enamel.

Blacken the tyre walls with some shoe polish.

Remove dead insects from the grill by applying a strong detergent or borax solution and allowing to soak for 5-10 minutes before scrubbing the grill with a pot brush.

Tar spots can be removed with a rag soaked in kerosene. Allow to soak before rubbing off the spots.

Use steel wool to rub rust and scale from chrome plating.

Chewed tapes

When your cassette player chews a tape, simply cut out the damaged part and join the free ends with a tiny piece of sticky tape.

You will only have lost a small part of the music, and it is better than discarding the tape.

Drying flowers and herbs

A small portable clothesline makes a good rack or base from which to hang bunches of herbs and flowers to dry.

Choose a dust free spot where air can circulate. Drying may take a week or so. Use the dried flowers in pot pourri or sachets.

Use dried flower heads of lavender and roses to make a scented pot pourri to fill attractive silver or glass bowls and scent your rooms. Add a fixative such as orris root and a little lavender or rose essential oil (available from specialist perfumeries) and leave the mixture to mature in a dark spot for a month or two in an airtight container.

Energy savers

You can cut your electricity bills by a few simple measures. Install dimmers, timers and thermostats to cut electricity costs.

Don't leave heaters on low at night; turn them off.

Use the dishwasher only when it's full.

Don't fill the kettle for just one drink; only boil as much as you need. Alternatively, boil enough water for the day's tea and coffee first thing in the morning, then store it in a thermos where it will keep warm for the rest of the day.

Entertaining

The first job when planning a party, no matter how simple or small, is to make a list.

Write down your guests (invited and accepted), your proposed menu and beverages, shopping list and what you need to do in the way of general preparation. Check that you have enough chairs, tables, crockery, cutlery, glassware, table linen and trays. Have you a reliable corkscrew and bottle opener?

Don't try to serve such elaborate food that you can't enjoy your guests' company and attend to other duties of a host — particularly if you are singlehanded.

Never try out new recipes on guests — experiment with your own family or close friends first.

Prepare as much as possible in advance. Choose a menu that allows you to cook at least one course the day before, perhaps a soup or dessert. Shop, set tables and do flowers the day or evening before, and organise the drinks on a bar.

Check your bathroom. Make sure it is looking attractive — clean, and with plenty of guest towels and soaps.

If you are entertaining large numbers, it's a good idea to get some professional advice on quantities of food and beverages you will need.

For informal gatherings of large numbers, let others share the work and bring a dish or a bottle of wine.

A baby's bath or your own bathtub filled with ice is an efficient way to keep drinks cool.

Six or eight are the most manageable numbers for sit-down dining — unless you have plenty of help.

Spend some time working out seating for sit-down dinners — who will get on with whom and so on.

Etiquette for formal dining

Cutlery on the table is always set so that the implements correspond to the courses of the meal. They are ranged in order, starting from the outside. Implements used in the right hand are on the right side of the place mat, those used in the left hand are on the left.

So if the first course is to be soup, the round soup spoon will be on the outside of the setting.

(There may be a bread-and-butter knife for use with bread outside it, or this may be on the bread and butter plate.)

Or if there is to be a fish course first, the fish knife and fork will be on the outside of the setting.

Forks in a place setting should be placed with their tines up, knives with their blades turned in towards the place mat.

Occasionally, the dessert spoon and fork are laid above the place mat.

When you are at a formal dinner and in doubt about which implement to use, follow your host's example.

The bread-and-butter plate is on the left of the setting, with the napkin on it or on or above the place mat.

The usual order of courses is a soup and/or entrée, main course, cheese and biscuits then dessert. Sometimes the dessert precedes the cheese.

If male, always draw out the chair of the women next to you and help them be seated before the meal.

Food is usually served from the left. Empty plates are taken from the right.

Do not start eating until everyone has been served and the host has started — unless you are asked to do so by the host. If you are the host, make sure you insist your guests eat while the food is hot!

When you have finished eating, leave your knife and fork together, the fork with the tines up, resting on the plate in front of you, with the ends of the implements over the edge.

Plates should not be removed from the table until everyone has finished eating.

Never stack dishes at the table. They should be carried to the kitchen in twos.

Wine glasses are set out slightly to the right of the place setting. As well as red and white wine, you may serve or be served a dry sherry with soup and a sweet dessert wine or champagne with dessert.

A dessert wine should be served in a small wine glass, champagne in flutes.

When eating soup, tip the spoon away from you and take the soup from the far side of the bowl. Tip the bowl away from you slightly to spoon up the last of the liquid.

If you are a guest, don't forget to thank your host both when you are leaving and with a note or telephone call in the following few days.

Do not smoke at the table until everyone has finished eating. Ask the host's permission as a courtesy.

Extension cords

A shoelace tied in a loop can make a handy sling for hanging up an extension cord.

Flower arranging

Crush the stems of woody plants before you arrange them.

A crushed aspirin in the water of cut flowers will make them last longer.

Always pick flowers early in the morning in hot weather.

If you pick them in the evening, plunge them up to their necks in cold water overnight.

Cut off all foliage below the water line in a vase of cut flowers to avoid polluting the water.

(The exception to this rule is lilac as the leaves act as a water conductor.)

Always have a low bowl of flowers on a dinner table. A high arrangement blocks the guests' vision and conversation.

Avoid highly perfumed flowers on meal tables. They can spoil the flavour and appreciation of both food and wine.

Strips of transparent sticky tape in rows across the top of the vase will keep flower arrangements in place.

To repair a leaking or porous vase, melt two tablespoons paraffin wax in a saucepan and thickly cover the inside bottom and sides of the vase with melted wax to the required depth. Allow the wax to dry. The coating will make the vase waterproof.

Garden hose

Coil your garden hose in a figure of eight. You will then be able to pull it out without coils or kinks.

Health

Remember that caffeine makes the skin sun-sensitive so don't drink tea, coffee or cola if you are out in the sun a lot.

Herbal tea such as chamomile is a mild soporific and good for the digestion. Drink it at night instead of tea and coffee, which are stimulants.

Water is the best natural laxative. Drink plenty of water every day for a good complexion and healthy system. Start each meal with at least one glass of water to avoid constipation.

If you are on a low-fat diet, use non-stick cookware to prepare your meals and season food with herbs or a little lemon juice instead of fat.

Regular exercise is essential to maintain fitness. It also reduces stress. Little and often — for example, a brisk half-hour walk every day — is a good way to start a fitness programme.

Evening primrose oil, available from chemists and supermarkets, will relieve the symptoms of pre-menstrual tension: irritability, fluid retention, fatigue and depression.

If you are a regular student, use a slanted desk to avoid back and neck strain.

Take time to learn the principles of good nutrition from an expert. Unless there are medical reasons to do otherwise, we should eat from the five basic food groups every day in the correct proportions: vegetables and fruit; cereals and pasta; dairy products; protein; fats and oils.

Herbs

Make a herb infusion to add to your bath. Pour boiling water over a handful of rosemary leaves or lavender flowers. Leave to stand for 10 minutes, strain and add the soothing and scented decoction to your bathwater.

You can also use it in a footbath for tired and aching feet.

Chew raw parsley to sweeten the breath. Parsley is also rich in vitamin C.

Chamomile tea aids the digestion and is a mild relaxant.

Soak rose hips in boiling water to make an infusion that is rich in vitamin C.

Drink rose-hip tea to ward off colds.

Herb and flower wreaths

Straw or foam wreath forms are available at florists and craft outlets. Use these as a base to attach fresh or dried herbs and flowers from your garden. Use florists' wire and pins to attach the material and finish with a loop of wire for hanging. You can use smaller forms to make wreaths to sit around candlestick bases on the table for a festive occasion.

Indoor plants

To test whether a plant needs watering, stick your finger in the soil. If the top centimetre is dry, then water the plant.

Always use room temperature water in plants, as cold water can kill them.

Keep plants well away from air-conditioners and heaters.

Sponge plants regularly with soapy water (not detergent) to remove dust and pests.

When you are going on holidays cover indoor plants with plastic bags, which will trap the moisture from evaporation.

Turn plants around at regular intervals so they don't lean towards light sources.

Keeping cool

If building a new house or undertaking major renovations, minimise windows on the western side and try to position the main living areas so that they face north.

Brick is a better insulator than weatherboard, but using light-coloured paints also helps to keep the inside cooler.

External shading provides the best heat protection. Trees are an obvious natural source of shade as well as having aesthetic appeal. Other possibilities are erecting pergolas made with shade cloth, blinds or wide eaves. Internal blinds are less effective because they allow the sun's rays to hit the window.

Insulate the ceiling. Insulation also helps to keep the house warmer in winter. Consider installing double-glazing, which helps to prevent the heat from penetrating. It also reduces drafts and dramatically reduces outside noise.

Ceiling fans are excellent except in extreme heat. Air-conditioning is the most effective mechanical means, although it is comparatively expensive and the noise of the machine bothers some people.

Keys

If your key is catching in the lock, try rubbing it with

a lead pencil. The graphite will smooth off the edges. This also works for zipper teeth that are sticking.

Lavender ideas

Make lavender sachets for your drawers and wardrobes from lace handkerchiefs. Lay the handkerchief flat, pile with a mixture of dried lavender, bay leaves and a little camphor and sprinkle with lavender oil. Gather the corners of the hand-kerchief together and tie with ribbon.

Moths hate the strong scent.

Lids

To loosen stuck lids on glass jars, run hot water around the screw top.

Another method is to invert the jar and gently knock it against a wooden bench top.
Use the handle of a kitchen spoon as a lever when opening tins with a key.

Moving house

In the process of moving house, keep a basket of essential items like coffee, tea, mugs, a jar of biscuits, a towel, torch, toilet paper, a beloved toy or two for children and essential medications.

Don't forget to arrange at the post office for your mail to be redirected to your new address.

When packing fragile items like china, remember that plates travel better stacked on edge sideways with newspaper between each one rather than flat on top of each other.

Mark all boxes clearly and indicate where they are to go in your new home. Tag furniture.

Before moving heavy appliances or furniture over polished or vinyl floors, slip an old folded blanket underneath to avoid marking the floor.

Make sure you have arranged to have newspapers, telephone, milk, gas and electricity services stopped or transferred.

Lift furniture and heavy objects correctly and avoid back and pelvic injury.

Don't bend from the waist. Squat and use your leg muscles to do the work.

Pantihose

Store bulbs in old pantihose. You can knot them and hang up in a dark airy spot.

A quick repair job for a run in stockings or pantihose is a dab of clear nail varnish or a rub with wet soap.

Use old pantihose to tie plants up in the garden —

they won't cut or bruise the plants.

If you wash pantihose in warm soapy water before use, they will last longer.

Plant labels

Make cheap, durable plant labels by cutting up a discarded plastic ice cream bucket.

Write the names with laundry marking pen or other waterproof marker.

Plant pots

Instead of using broken crocks in the bottom of plant pots, a piece of plastic fly screen or shade cloth is easier and more effective.

Records

Before playing black vinyl records, wipe the surface clean with a soft, wet rag, preferably either chamois leather or optical cleaning cloth.

Saving water

Fix leaking taps and toilets. A steady drip can waste thousands of litres a year.

Install a flow-restricting shower rose.

Sweep leaves away instead of hosing them.

Put a timer on your sprinkler.

Security at home

Don't forget to cancel newspapers and milk when

you go away. Arrange for your mail to be diverted or for a neighbour to collect it.

Keep the shrubs and trees trimmed back from your house — foliage can hide intruders.

Make sure you have adequate outside lighting.

Don't leave lights on day and night when you go away. An electric timer will turn lights on and off at different times to foil possible intruders.

Never leave keys secreted outside.

Make sure you have a door viewer on your front door that will allow you to screen visitors. A chain lock means extra security.

Check that your doors and windows are all satisfactorily secure. Doors should have a deadlock system, ground floor windows should have key lockable bolts. Keys to windows should be readily accessible in case of fire.

Glass-panelled doors are easily entered. An intruder simply breaks the glass near the handle, puts a hand in and unlatches the door from the inside.

Install bars on glass doors or replace them with ones of solid construction.

Sheepskin boots

Don't discard worn sheepskin boots; cut them up and use pieces of lambswool for shoe polishing pads.

They are also good for dusting awkward areas around the dashboard and central console of your car.

Storage ideas

When stowing suitcases away, put a cake of scented soap in the cases to fend off musty smells.

Don't waste empty space under beds. Turn them into storage areas. Use flat boxes or containers — on castors if possible, so that you can slide them in and out easily.

Use your shower or bath to stow wet umbrellas or raincoats. They can drip off without making a mess.

Store woollens in plastic bags with lavender sachets to protect them against moths.

Don't waste empty space in the top compartment of wardrobes and built-in cupboards. Have an extra shelf inserted to give you more storage room.

Fix plasticised kitchen racks such as spice racks inside your bathroom or dresser doors. These make good makeup and bottle storage areas.

Never stack paintings on top of each other — they must have room for air to circulate between them. Arrange them leaning against a wall.

Here's a clever idea to show off articles such as brushes and makeup pencils on your dressing table or in the bathroom.

Buy a cup or so of tiny silver ball bearings from the hardware store and pour them into a clear plastic container or glass vase.

Push the handles of your toilet articles into the bearings, which will hold them upright. Or you could use a small cane basket filled with pretty pebbles.

Wine

Sherry (dry or medium) is good with soups and hors d'oeuvres. It can be served chilled in summer.

Dry and medium white wines go well with fish and shellfish, salads, chicken and cold dishes. Serve chilled.

Red wines — heavy or light — are all good with red meat, roast poultry, cheese or game. Serve at room temperature.

Sweet or fruity white wines are best with dessert or sweet fresh fruit. Serve chilled.

Port and Madeira go with cheese or fruit. Serve at room temperature.

Champagne is an appetiser, good with hors d'oeuvres, seafood or desserts. Serve chilled.

Rosé is a good wine to serve with lunch or dessert. It's slightly sweet. Serve chilled.

Store your wine in an area away from vibration which could shake the sediment.

If possible, wine should be stored in a dark area where the temperature is constant and cool.

Bottled wine should be stored on its side so that the wine is against the cork and helps the sealing process.

A moist cork is easier to remove than a dry one which could break.

If you buy wines in cartons, simply turn them on their sides to store.
It's generally agreed these days that it is not necessary to open red wines hours before drinking them to let them 'breathe', as wine in fact starts to oxidise as soon as it is exposed to the air.

Similarly, most wines these days don't have to be decanted. If you buy an old wine you may wish to decant it to get rid of the sediment — but don't let the wine stand too long once you have opened it as exposure to the air may spoil the wine.

The acid in vinegar and, to a lesser extent, lemon juice can temporarily spoil the palate so that wine is not appreciated. Keep this in mind when planning a menu.

Don't have highly-perfumed flowers in table decorations. The scent can spoil the palate.

VOLUME MEASURES

Standard measure	Imperial	Metric
1 teaspoon	$\frac{1}{8}$ fl oz	5 ml
2 teaspoons	$\frac{1}{4}$ fl oz	10 ml
1 tablespoon	$\frac{1}{2}$ fl oz	20 ml
1$\frac{1}{2}$ tablespoons	1 fl oz	30 ml
2 tablespoons		40 ml
2$\frac{1}{2}$ tablespoons	1$\frac{1}{2}$ fl oz	50 ml
3 tablespoons	2 fl oz	60 ml
4 tablespoons		80 ml
5 tablespoons	3 fl oz	100 ml
$\frac{1}{2}$ cup	4 fl oz	125 ml
7$\frac{1}{2}$ tablespoons	5 fl oz	150 ml
1 cup	8 fl oz	250 ml
1$\frac{1}{2}$ cups	12 fl oz	375 ml
2 cups	16 fl oz	500 ml
2$\frac{1}{2}$ cups	20 fl oz/1 pint	625 ml
5 cups	40 fl oz	1.25 litres

LENGTH MEASURES

Imperial	Metric
1/4 inch	5 mm
1/2 inch	10 mm/1 cm
3/4 inch	20 mm/2 cm
1 inch	25 mm/2.5 cm
1 1/2 inches	40 mm/4 cm
2 inches	50 mm/5 cm
4 inches	100 mm/10 cm
6 inches	150 mm/15 cm
12 inches/1 foot	300 mm/30 cm
18 inches	450 mm/45 cm

WEIGHT MEASURES

Imperial	Metric
½ oz	15 g
1 oz	30 g
2 oz	60 g
3 oz	90 g
4 oz	125 g
8 oz/½ lb	250 g
10 oz	315 g
12 oz	375 g
16 oz/1 lb	500 g
24 oz/1½ lb	750 g
32 oz/2 lb	1000 g/1 kg

DAILY CALORIE REQUIREMENTS

Woman with desk job	2000 Calories
Woman with active job (e.g. housewife, teacher)	2300 Calories
Man with desk job	2500 Calories
Man with active job (e.g. tradesman, teacher)	2800 Calories
Man with very active job (e.g. labourer)	3300 Calories
Professional athlete (male or female)	Up to 4000 Calories

CALORIE COUNTER

Average serving	Calorie count
Bread and cereals	
White bread, 1 slice	65
Wholemeal bread, 1 slice	55
Rice, 1 cup	200
Drinks	
Carbonated drinks	105
Milk, whole, 1 cup	165
Milk, skim, 1 cup	90
Dairy foods	
Butter, 1 teaspoon	100
Cheddar cheese, 30 g	115
Cottage cheese, 1 cup	240
Cream, unsweetened, 1 teaspoon	25
Egg	80

CALORIE COUNTER

Average serving	*Calorie count*
Desserts	
Pie, custard, 1 slice	265
Pie, fruit, 1 slice	340
Cake	variable
Chocolate slice	295
Ice cream, plain	150
Fruit	
Apple, raw	70
Banana	85
Grapefruit, half	40
Orange	70
Peach, raw	35
Pineapple, canned, 1 slice	95
Fruit juice	
Orange, fresh, 1 cup	105
Tomato, canned, 1 cup	50

CALORIE COUNTER

Average serving	Calorie count
Vegetables	
Broccoli, 1 cup	70
Carrots, 1 cup	45
Peas, 1 cup	65
Potatoes, mashed, 1 cup	110
Spinach, 1 cup	45
Tomato, raw, 1 cup	30
Meat, fish and poultry	
Beef, steak, 250 g	375
Lamb chop, 100 g	450
Pork chop, 100g	295
Ham, 100 g	340
Bacon, 2 slices	95
Sardines, 100 g	180
Salmon, canned, 100 g	120

HOUSEHOLD HINTS

❖

Mildew in the bathroom? Need to mend a fuse? What's the best way to open a paint tin? This collection of practical hints provides answers to hundreds of common household problems. Here are tips on stain removal, cleaning and laundering, child safety, accident prevention, home maintenance, decorating, sewing, entertaining, first aid and pet care.

You won't have to spend a fortune on costly, environment-threatening chemicals or aerosols. The solutions here rely on inexpensive household cleaning items that have stood the test of time.

ISBN 0-09-182807-4

9 780091 828073

RANDOM LITTLE LIBRARY